THE STATE OF

YOUTH

MINISTRY

How Churches Reach Today's Teens— and What Parents Think About It

A Barna Report Produced in Partnership with Youth Specialties and YouthWorks

CONTENTS

PREFACE

BY YOUTH SPECIALTIES AND YOUTHWORKS

Church youth ministry is a young practice, and one that is often conducted in relative isolation from the church body and broader community. It can be hard to know if what you are doing is similar to or totally different from other leaders around the country. Perhaps you have wondered, *Are we all struggling with the same issue or am I the only one?*

The reality is, you are not alone. Across the country, thousands of student ministry leaders are seeking to effectively reach a new generation of teenagers. Shifts in youth culture are only part of the equation. Changes over the last decade have disrupted the status quo of institutions throughout America and across the globe. Not surprisingly, these changes have impacted churches and youth ministries as well. It's our job to ask *How?* and *Why?* and *What now?*

But none of us can adequately answer these questions on our own.

Regardless of your level of experience, operating based only on your own perspective—or even on the perspectives of a handful of practitioners—can leave you with a narrow narrative. It's important not to limit your knowledge to anecdotal evidence.

For years various organizations (including Youth Specialties and YouthWorks) have brought together youth pastors to learn, share and create, but we've been missing objective research on how churches actually do youth ministry and whether what they're doing is effective—and why. We need a wider view of what's happening in youth ministry in America; not a peephole, but a picture window into what is working and what is not.

In 2013, Youth Specialties and YouthWorks partnered with Barna to launch a study of several areas of youth ministry. We

WE NEED A WIDER VIEW OF WHAT'S HAPPENING IN YOUTH MINISTRY IN AMERICA; NOT A PEEPHOLE, BUT A PICTURE WINDOW INTO WHAT IS WORKING AND WHAT IS NOT

asked questions to understand how youth pastors and senior pastors view their student ministry. We wondered if senior pastors' views differ from those of youth pastors, and in what ways. Surprisingly, we found a more optimistic outlook than what we'd been hearing at our conferences and events.

In 2016, we commissioned Barna to conduct a second wave of research to see if perspectives had changed. In addition to tracking the questions asked of pastors three years ago, we also wanted to gather data on parents' perspectives and on attitudes about student service and mission. Collecting this second set of data would allow Barna researchers and our teams to track change over time and come away with new insights on the state of youth ministry in America.

What you'll find in the following pages is a wider view of the youth ministry landscape—our numbers, our values and our hopes, as well as the challenges we face now and believe are coming in the near future. We hope this report offers not only information but also wisdom that will spark conversations and lead to more effective student ministries, healthier youth workers and, ultimately, stronger churches and sturdier teen faith.

Most of all, we hope you gain an overwhelming sense that you are not alone in your ministry to teenagers. Although we each serve in our own context, we are pursuing, pastoring and pointing a new generation toward Jesus together.

WE HOPE THIS REPORT OFFERS NOT ONLY INFORMATION BUT ALSO WISDOM THAT WILL SPARK CONVERSATIONS

INTRODUCTION

It could be said that the first youth group was formed when Jesus called his disciples to follow him. And from that youth group, the Church was born.

Youth ministry has certainly changed since the first century. The Church and society have changed, and the young embrace those changes most readily. When we consider that, for many of us, the older we get the less we look forward to change, it's no surprise youth ministers often feel it more acutely than others in ministry. They can't escape it. The youth hunger for it, instigate it, always ask why—and our youth leaders have the shepherd calling to do as Jesus did with his first recruits: help them follow his way as the world changes around them.

Youth pastors, more often than most other ministry positions, deal with diverse people in the church, each of whom has their own set of expectations. There is the senior pastor to please, parents to please and the teenagers themselves (who aren't, as a rule, known for being easy to please). Meeting the expectations of all three groups—and of other folks we didn't mention, like the church custodian, who in some cases has more clout and influence than the youth minister—can be a daunting challenge.

This report is a side-by-side snapshot of how well senior pastors' and parents' expectations and perceptions of the youth program line up with their youth pastor's. (We left out the custodian.)

Some leaders picking up this report will crack it open with trepidation. *I can't take any more bad news,* they might think—and their fear would be understandable. Over the past decade, youth ministry has been relentlessly critiqued both from within its ranks and from without. That kind of persistent criticism can be demoralizing and exhausting.

But this report is not another critique. It's simply a survey of the state of youth ministry in churches across the America—and the sheer volume of good news may surprise you.

If you have a group of twelve kids who don't understand your illustrations and one of them wants to kill you, you have a youth group like Jesus.

MARK YACONELLI,
WRITER, SPEAKER, YOUTH LEADER

For one thing, parents and youth pastors are on a similar wavelength when it comes to assessing the health and effectiveness of their youth ministry. The vast majority of youth pastors says their program is healthy (56%) or somewhat healthy (38%), and more than nine out of 10 parents say their church's youth ministry is very (53%) or somewhat effective (40%).

And that's not all. Youth leaders' goals and priorities for their ministry are closely aligned with their senior pastor's, as you'll see in Part One. And both groups of leaders are hopeful about the future. For example, a significant majority of senior pastors say they do not anticipate replacing their paid youth pastor with a volunteer—a trend some feared would gain ground—and many say they plan to transition the current volunteer position to paid ministry staff.

In Part Two you'll find data on what youth groups are actually doing: discipleship strategies, small vs. large group formats, use of curriculum and outside resources, and outreach (or lack thereof) to teens outside the church.

Part Three examines how leaders and parents think about service and mission trips as an aspect of the youth program: their purpose, effectiveness and significance for the goals of youth ministry and for the mission of the Church.

The subtitle of this report is "How Churches Reach Today's Teens—and What Parents Think About It." One reading of this might indicate a potentially adversarial relationship between church leaders and parents. But we believe the data in *The State of Youth Ministry* can actually help parents and pastors get on the same page when it comes to helping teens follow the way of Jesus. If we understand each other's hopes and expectations, we can work better together to make young disciples who will lead the Church into an uncertain future.

Our teenagers are counting on us.

PART ONE

THE WHY OF YOUTH MINISTRY

We could think about the conversation concerning youth ministry that is taking place across the Church in North America as a macrocosm of the personal, everyday conversations in each local church: between senior pastor and youth pastor, youth pastor and parent, parent and student and so on. Each party holds their own assumptions and expectations about what youth ministry should be and why, as well as their own metrics for determining its success.

Part One examines how pastors, youth leaders and parents understand the goals and priorities, strengths and challenges of their church's ministry to youth—and what the differences mean for the overall health of the youth program.

THE RELATIONSHIP BETWEEN ◄ ·············

PARENT PERCEPTIONS

"I am familiar with my teen's youth program."

 56% Very familiar

31% Somewhat familiar

11% Not that familiar

n=295 U.S. parents of teens who regularly attend youth group | Feb. 2016

"I am very concerned with the social functions of a youth ministry."

Say it's very important that the youth program ...

 **69**%

Is a safe space to explore faith

 **67**%

Provides positive peer relationships

 **58**%

Is a place where teens can bring friends

Expect that the youth pastor will ...

 **62**%

Help teens navigate friendships

 **60**%

Help teens navigate family relationships

"I am satisfied with my teen's youth ministry—and its minister."

 93% Feel the youth group is "somewhat" or "very" effective

 95% Are "somewhat" or "very" satisfied with the youth pastor

"I generally know the youth pastor."

 **45**%

Interact with the youth pastor a lot—which also increases satisfaction levels

PARENTS & YOUTH LEADERS

LEADER PERCEPTIONS

"I would like more parents to be engaged with my youth ministry."

23%
Say getting more parents involved in spiritual formation is a goal

34%
Identify a lack of parent interest as a challenge

74%
of youth pastors say teen busyness is the main obstacle to ministry

MEANWHILE

"I wish your teen wasn't so busy."

31%
of parents think their teen needs more to do

11%
of parents think their child is way too busy

"Your family dynamic might also affect my ministry."

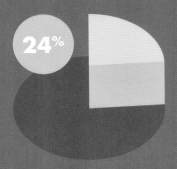

24%

See the breakdown of families as a top challenge

"I am optimistic about getting more families involved."

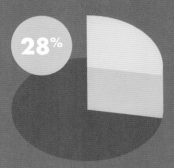

28%

Believe they'll have more families involved in the next three years

n=352 U.S. youth pastors | n=295 U.S. parents of teens who regularly attend youth group | Feb. 2016

1.

GOALS & PRIORITIES

There is a persistent notion that senior pastors and youth ministers often don't see eye to eye on aims and outcomes of their youth department. Barna researchers, however, found evidence to the contrary: Senior pastors and youth leaders are generally aligned when it comes to their thinking about what youth ministry should accomplish.

When they are asked to identify the top two goals of youth ministry, a substantial majority of church leaders choose "discipleship and spiritual instruction" as one of their highest priorities. Seven in 10 senior pastors (71%) and three-quarters of youth pastors (75%) say this is one of their top goals.

"Building relationships with students" is a primary objective for about half of youth pastors (48%) and two in five senior pastors (40%), while "evangelism and outreach to youth" is selected by roughly one-quarter of each group (29% senior pastors, 24% youth pastors). "Evangelism to the parents of teens," on the other hand, does not appear to be as important (7% senior pastors, 4% among youth pastors).

Even if most church leaders don't prioritize reaching out to parents, many express a hope that parents will reach *in*. One in six senior pastors believe "getting parents involved with spiritual formation" is a top goal of youth ministry (18%). And youth pastors are even more likely to say so: One-quarter identifies this as a priority for their ministry (23%).

Similar percentages of senior pastors (12%) and youth pastors (10%) feel that providing a "safe and nurturing environment"

SENIOR PASTORS AND YOUTH LEADERS ARE GENERALLY ALIGNED WHEN IT COMES TO WHAT YOUTH MINISTRY SHOULD ACCOMPLISH

is an important goal. (As we will see, this is a much higher priority among parents.)

Senior pastors (17%) are more likely than youth pastors (10%) to emphasize "serving the community"—but "serving the church body" is at the bottom of both groups' lists (6% senior pastors and 4% youth pastors).

GOALS OF YOUTH MINISTRY: SENIOR PASTORS & YOUTH PASTORS

● senior pastors ● youth pastors

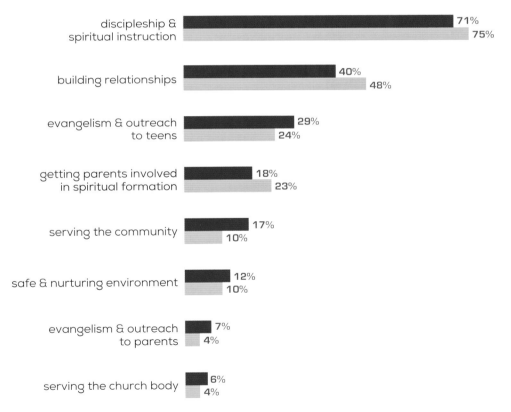

discipleship & spiritual instruction
71%
75%

building relationships
40%
48%

evangelism & outreach to teens
29%
24%

getting parents involved in spiritual formation
18%
23%

serving the community
17%
10%

safe & nurturing environment
12%
10%

evangelism & outreach to parents
7%
4%

serving the church body
6%
4%

Feb. 2016, n=381 U.S. senior pastors, n=352 U.S. youth pastors.

Overall, senior pastors and youth pastors are in sync when it comes to the goals of youth ministry, but there are notable differences when researchers segment these groups by church location, size and denomination, and by the pastor's ethnicity.

For example, discipleship—chosen by a significant majority of all senior and youth pastors—is not as important to youth ministers in urban churches (59%) as it is to those in small towns (84%) or the suburbs (76%). Similarly, senior pastors of mainline congregations (58% vs. 75% non-mainline) are less likely to list discipleship as one of their top goals. On the other hand, white youth leaders (78%) are more inclined than those of other ethnicities (51%) to say discipleship is a driving force of their youth ministry.

Elsewhere, serving the community and the church proves to be of higher importance. Pastors of urban churches (31% vs. 13% of those in other communities), Hispanic (25%) and black (34%) youth pastors (vs. 11% white), and youth leaders in mainline congregations (18% vs. 12% non-mainline) are more likely to list one or both of the service-oriented goals as a top priority.

Senior pastors of mainline churches (61%) are more likely than non-mainline pastors (32%) to say building relationships with students is a top goal, and female youth pastors (63%) are likewise more inclined than their male counterparts (44%) to choose this option. (Mainline congregations are more likely to have a female youth pastor, so sometimes it's unclear whether denomination or gender is a determining factor.)

PRIORITIZING DISCIPLESHIP & OUTREACH

Discipleship is a primary goal for three out of four youth pastors—but not all of them define discipleship the same way.

Offered a list of options, youth leaders could choose one or more phrases they believe accurately describe the goal of discipleship. Barna found that, generally speaking, youth pastors tend to favor definitions that are somewhat nebulous and difficult to quantify, and rank lower the options that can be measured with some level of accuracy. For example, "being transformed to become more like Jesus," preferred by nearly eight out of 10 youth leaders (78%), certainly has robust biblical support but, at the same time, is hard to measure. On the other hand, it seems comparatively easy to assess more concrete goals such as "being mentored in Christian maturity" (56%) or "winning new believers to follow Christ" (32%)—both of which, it might be argued, are components of becoming "more like Jesus." (The chart highlights the discipleship goals that might be fairly easy to quantify—all three are at or near the bottom of the preference list.)

Given the difficulty of quantifying success, youth pastors might consider how to think strategically, not only aspirationally, about their discipleship goals—or at least about how to assess whether they are reaching those goals.

YOUTH PASTORS SHOULD CONSIDER HOW TO THINK STRATEGICALLY, NOT ONLY ASPIRATIONALLY, ABOUT THEIR DISCIPLESHIP GOALS

THE GOAL OF DISCIPLESHIP: YOUTH PASTORS

being transformed to become more like Jesus	78%
growing in spiritual maturity	76%
knowing Christ more deeply	69%
learning to live a more consistent Christian life	64%
learning to trust God more	57%
being mentored in Christian maturity	56%
deepening faith through education & fellowship	55%
becoming more obedient to God	48%
winning new believers to follow Jesus Christ	32%

Feb. 2016. n=352 U.S. youth pastors.

Discipleship is high on most youth pastors' priority list, but a small majority also says that reaching teens outside the church is a significant focus of their ministry. About one in seven reports their church places "a lot" of emphasis on outreach to teens (13%), while two in five report "some" emphasis on reaching out (41%). The remaining 46 percent say outreach to teens outside the church is "a little" (37%) or "not at all" (9%) an emphasis for their congregation.

LEVEL OF SIGNIFICANCE CHURCH PLACES ON OUTREACH TO TEENS: YOUTH PASTORS

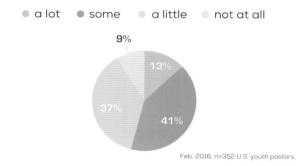

● a lot ● some ● a little ● not at all

Feb. 2016, *n*=352 U.S. youth pastors.

Female youth pastors (42%) are less likely than their male colleagues (56%) to say outreach is a significant emphasis of their ministry (perhaps because, as we saw in their top two goals, they are more focused on building strong relationships within the existing youth group). On the other hand, leaders whose youth groups are on the larger side (21% vs. 9% leaders of fewer than 50 students) and pastors of non-mainline churches (62% vs. 38% mainline) are more likely to say reaching teens outside the church is highly significant for their church.

OUTLINING PARENT EXPECTATIONS

Parents have their own set of priorities when it comes to their kids' youth-ministry experience. And, as the chart shows, most parents have a hard time narrowing them down! A majority of parents whose teens regularly attend youth group rate each and every feature as either "very" or "somewhat important."

Safety is of paramount importance to virtually all parents (96% very + somewhat important). Presumably this would include their kids being kept safe from physical harm, but many parents may also think of safety in emotional terms, especially since the phrase "safe space" is common jargon today for a group in which a person feels emotionally secure.

Essentially, parents want a supportive community for their kids where they have positive friendships with peers who are also exploring faith.

Notably, while "outreach to teens who do not attend church" ranks low on the list of parent priorities, nine out of 10 say it is very (51%) or somewhat important (39%) to them. Like youth pastors, parents acknowledge that outreach and evangelism are important—but not *as* important as their other priorities.

PARENTS WANT A SUPPORTIVE COMMUNITY FOR THEIR KIDS WHERE THEY HAVE POSITIVE FRIENDSHIPS WITH PEERS WHO ARE EXPLORING FAITH

PARENT PRIORITIES FOR THE YOUTH PROGRAM

% "very" or "somewhat" important among U.S. parents whose teens regularly attend youth group

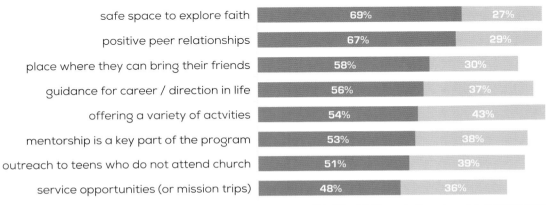

● very important   ◌ somewhat important

	very important	somewhat important
safe space to explore faith	69%	27%
positive peer relationships	67%	29%
place where they can bring their friends	58%	30%
guidance for career / direction in life	56%	37%
offering a variety of actvities	54%	43%
mentorship is a key part of the program	53%	38%
outreach to teens who do not attend church	51%	39%
service opportunities (or mission trips)	48%	36%

Feb. 2016, n=295 U.S. parents of teens who regularly attend youth group.

Youth pastors significantly shape the group experience, and parents' expectations of their leaders reflect that reality. Seven in 10 parents whose teen regularly attends youth group say they have a "major expectation" that their youth pastor is "discipling teens" (72%). This majority expectation appears to align with church leaders' goals for youth ministry (yet it's an open question whether parents and pastors share a definition of discipleship). About six in 10 parents say youth leaders should be "helping [teens] navigate friend relationships" (62%) and "helping them navigate family relationships" (60%), which may point to the relational volatility so many teens—and, by virtue of proximity, their parents!—experience as they proceed through adolescence.

White (47% vs. 30% other ethnicities) and high-income parents (52% vs. 36% less than $100K per year) are more likely than others to say "talking about sexuality and dating" is a major expectation, while lower-income parents are inclined to say they expect youth pastors to help their teen navigate family relationships (71% vs. 56% more than $50K per year) and warn them about drugs and alcohol (72% vs. 50%).

PARENT EXPECTATIONS OF THE YOUTH PASTOR

% "major expectation" among U.S. parents whose teen regularly attends youth group

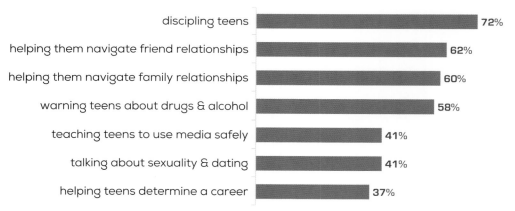

discipling teens	72%
helping them navigate friend relationships	62%
helping them navigate family relationships	60%
warning teens about drugs & alcohol	58%
teaching teens to use media safely	41%
talking about sexuality & dating	41%
helping teens determine a career	37%

Feb. 2016, *n*=295 U.S. parents of teens who regularly attend youth group.

Q&A WITH TERRY LINHART

Q: How can youth ministries harness and nurture young people who are already beginning to feel a call to ministry during their teen years?

A: I like to use the analogy of a baseball team that works to develop players through the minor leagues. Those of us in Christian ministry need to be scouting for students who show the interest, desire or skills for ministry. If God is calling them, then he has already gifted them for his work. So, like a baseball scout, we first keep an eye out for those young people who talk and act in ministerial ways. We need to watch our people, noticing moments where someone is clearly speaking or acting in ways that nurture others spiritually and otherwise.

Second, we need to have a plan to let students "try on" ministry. It used to be that all youth ministries had student leadership teams and held special training and events just for them. That's less common now, for various reasons, so there's less of an emphasis on leadership within youth ministries, beyond getting young people to help set up or promote an event. We need to find new ways to let young people exercise their gifts and create a nurturing space for God to affirm his call. When we let youth help lead, teach, counsel, coordinate and plan, they can "try on" ministry and get a glimpse of what their future may be.

Q: What do you consider to be trademarks of effective youth discipleship? What is unique about this season in a young person's life, and how should this influence the tone and content of spiritual instruction?

A: There are three characteristics that a discipling youth ministry should have. First, it must be a ministry with people who

TERRY LINHART
Educator, speaker and author

Terry Linhart, PhD, is professor of Christian ministries at Bethel College in Mishawaka, Indiana. A speaker and consultant, he is the author of seven books. Terry directs the Academic Support Network for Youth Specialties. He is the founder of the Arbor Research Group, a consulting firm that provides unique research and support to national and international Christian organizations.

www.TerryLinhart.com

pray. No programmatic trick or personal skill disciples; God is the one who transforms lives. We are about his business, not the other way around.

Second, a discipling ministry challenges students in appropriate ways. There is no shaming or authoritarianism—elements too common in programs for young people, even Christian ones. Rather, there is a teaching-centered ministry that is dynamic, relevant and focused on helping students serve and minister to others. It is a community where the message is clear and the community is warm and inviting.

The third and final element may be the most crucial: A discipling ministry, no matter how big it is, has a "life-on-life" aspect to its adult-student relationships. Biblical discipleship is not programmatic, but up-close and shared. It's not private, but communal. A young person's primary avenue for learning is social. They watch others and then learn in relationship through the modeling of adults and through conversations that explain the "why" behind what was observed. If adult leaders are close enough for young people to see them live out a Christ-centered faith, then there is greater opportunity for learning, for spiritual growth and faithfulness, for direction and redirection, and for support during difficulties.

BIBLICAL DISCIPLESHIP IS NOT PROGRAMMATIC, BUT UP-CLOSE AND SHARED. IT'S NOT PRIVATE, BUT COMMUNAL

Q: There can sometimes be this idea that youth ministry is the "junior varsity," a stepping stone to ministering to adults. How would you encourage pastors and leaders to combat this idea or, when fitting, to personally embrace a long-term calling to reaching this age group?

A: In my current role as a college professor, my weekly frustration is with those who don't think a person can have a lifetime career as a youth pastor. Many Christian parents, people who dearly love and trust God, talk their own children out of answering his call because of fear, embarrassment or lack of trust. The hesitation is usually economic, whether their son or daughter can earn a decent living as a full-time youth worker.

Their fear is whether getting a degree in Christian ministries is wise stewardship for the money they are investing in a college education. It is.

The church has learned some language about youth ministry from the 1980s that it needs to unlearn, especially with regard to ministry to middle school students. It's rare that, when a volunteer in the youth ministry is interviewed in a Sunday service, there isn't a joke made similar to "*Why* would anyone want to volunteer with middle school youth ministry?" or "You're a brave person to spend time with teenagers." That's leftover language that we need to toss out because it's gone stale.

As a church, as a community and even as a country, we need to value, support and champion ministry to young people, instead of throwing up our hands because the problems seem large or our own energy level is low. We need to marshal resources to find creative ways to empower and enable those who are called by God to serve and lead in ministry.

This is largely related to salary and benefits. The reality is that older youth workers are way more effective in youth ministry, but the way we've structured salaries and supervision is pushing them out. And we pay the price by looking for the next inexperienced youth worker every two to three years at many churches. Our financial investment (or lack thereof) reveals what we think of youth ministry.

If leaders and organizations would up their financial investment in youth ministry, the returns would be compounded. Not only would the ministry have a maturity and effectiveness that would speak volumes to families and the community, but other adults who volunteer with the youth ministry would be developed and trained to go out and lead. The entire church would benefit and flourish.

OUR FINANCIAL INVESTMENT (OR LACK THEREOF) REVEALS WHAT WE THINK OF YOUTH MINISTRY

2.

STRENGTHS & CHALLENGES

Setting goals and working toward hoped-for outcomes in teens' lives is well and good, but how do you know if you've hit the mark? Assessing the program's strengths and challenges is just as important as setting benchmarks of success.

Barna asked senior pastors to rate the strengths of their church's youth program on a sliding scale, from very strong on "reaching teens outside the church" to very strong on "discipling teens already in the church," and from very strong on "large group activities" to very strong on "small group activities." Most senior pastors place their church on the "discipling teens" and "small group" ends of the strengths scale.

Compared to non-mainline pastors (15%), mainline senior leaders (25%) tend to see outreach as a strength of their youth program (this belief is at odds with mainline youth pastors' self-assessments). Senior pastors of churches with at least one paid youth ministry staff member also consider outreach a strength (21% vs. 9% no paid staff). These same leaders are more likely than churches without paid youth staff to rate large group activities as a strength (31% vs. 18%), while senior pastors in urban churches (30%), on the other hand, have a greater tendency than pastors in other communities (11%) to say their program is strong when it comes to small group activities.

In some ways, senior pastors are outside the youth program looking in. So how do their assessments of the program's strengths align with youth pastors', who are on the inside looking around?

STRENGTHS OF THE YOUTH PROGRAM: SENIOR PASTORS

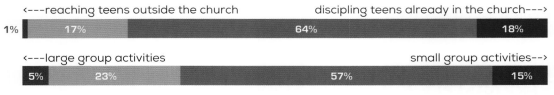

<---reaching teens outside the church   discipling teens already in the church--->

| 1% | 17% | 64% | 18% |

<---large group activities   small group activities-->

| 5% | 23% | 57% | 15% |

Feb. 2016, *n*=381 U.S. senior pastors.

Pretty closely, it turns out. Barna asked youth pastors to assess their own strengths on a sliding scale from very strong on "reaching teens outside the church" to very strong on "discipleship / mentoring programs," and their ministry preference from "large group" to "small group." Their self-reporting scale looks fairly similar to the senior pastors' strengths assessment.

Compared to male leaders (26%), female youth pastors (46%) are more likely to rate themselves as very strong on discipleship / mentoring. And when it comes to ministry preference, youth leaders over the age of 36 (23% vs. 14% younger leaders) and black youth pastors (30% vs. 17% all others) more strongly prefer small groups.

Overall, senior pastors' and youth ministers' assessments of the program match up. Most churches are more focused on discipling teens inside the church than on reaching teens outside the church, and tend to emphasize small group interactions over large

YOUTH PASTORS' STRENGTHS & PREFERENCES: SELF-ASSESSMENT

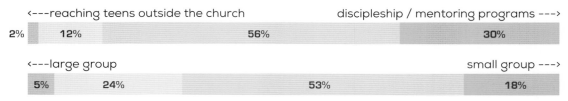

<---reaching teens outside the church   discipleship / mentoring programs --->

| 2% | 12% | 56% | 30% |

<---large group   small group --->

| 5% | 24% | 53% | 18% |

Feb. 2016, *n*=352 U.S. youth pastors.

group activities. Given that both types of leaders overwhelmingly see discipling and spiritual instruction as the goal of youth ministry, these findings are in line with expectations.

MEETING PARENT EXPECTATIONS

Parents were also given an opportunity to rate the strength of their church's youth program; researchers then overlaid parents' strength ratings with their self-reported priorities for the program. The resulting comparison looks like this:

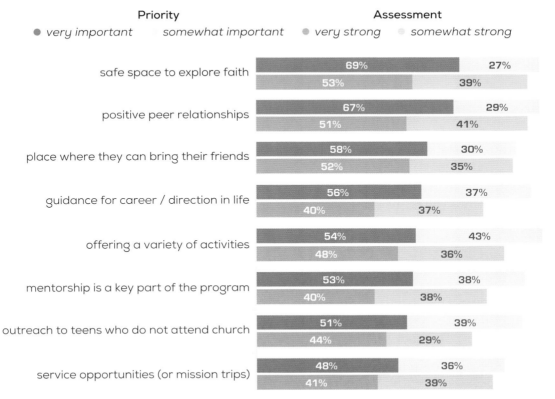

PARENT PRIORITIES & ASSESSMENT OF YOUTH PROGRAM STRENGTHS
% among U.S. parents whose teens regularly attend youth group

Priority
● very important   somewhat important

Assessment
● very strong   somewhat strong

	Priority	Assessment
safe space to explore faith	69%	27%
	53%	39%
positive peer relationships	67%	29%
	51%	41%
place where they can bring their friends	58%	30%
	52%	35%
guidance for career / direction in life	56%	37%
	40%	37%
offering a variety of activities	54%	43%
	48%	36%
mentorship is a key part of the program	53%	38%
	40%	38%
outreach to teens who do not attend church	51%	39%
	44%	29%
service opportunities (or mission trips)	48%	36%
	41%	39%

Feb. 2016, n=295 U.S. parents of teens who regularly attend youth group.

A majority of parents rate their church's program as "very strong" on only the top three priorities, and on a few of the priorities there is a substantial gap between parent expectations and their strength assessment. For example, the gap between "very important" and "very strong" for positive peer relationships and guidance for career / direction in life is 16 percentage points, and is 16 points for safe space to explore faith.

Still, more than two-thirds of parents say their program is at least somewhat strong in each of the priorities—a proportion that is on par with parents' overall satisfaction. Given an opportunity to rate their satisfaction with their church's youth ministry, more than nine out of 10 parents whose teen attends regularly report they are "very" (57%) or "somewhat satisfied" (39%). And similar proportions say their teen is "very" (58%) or "somewhat satisfied" (39%).

Parents are also overwhelmingly satisfied with their youth leader: More than nine out of 10 say they are "very" (59%) or "somewhat satisfied" (36%) with her or him. Interestingly, a high level of satisfaction with the youth leader correlates to more interaction between the parent and the leader. Nearly half of parents report "a lot" of interaction with the youth pastor (45%), and these highly involved parents are more likely to be "very satisfied" with their youth ministry leader (62% vs. 39% with less interaction). So, if parents in your program seem dissatisfied, consider asking them to volunteer!

Among parents whose teens regularly attend youth group, a majority says they are "very satisfied" with their youth pastor's performance in all but one area (47% administration / organization). Generally speaking, youth pastors are rated most highly on personal / character measures and lower on operations. (The exception in this category is "keeps kids safe"; three-quarters of parents are very satisfied with their youth pastor in this area.)

Roughly seven in 10 parents say they are very satisfied with their youth pastor as a "role model" (75%), with his or her

PARENTS ARE
OVERWHELMINGLY
SATISFIED WITH THEIR
YOUTH LEADER

PARENT SATISFACTION WITH YOUTH PASTOR'S PERFORMANCE

% "very satisfied" among U.S. parents whose teen regularly attends youth group

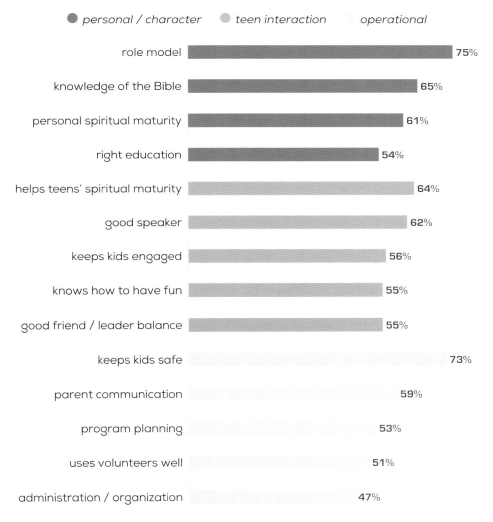

● personal / character   ● teen interaction   operational

role model	75%
knowledge of the Bible	65%
personal spiritual maturity	61%
right education	54%
helps teens' spiritual maturity	64%
good speaker	62%
keeps kids engaged	56%
knows how to have fun	55%
good friend / leader balance	55%
keeps kids safe	73%
parent communication	59%
program planning	53%
uses volunteers well	51%
administration / organization	47%

Feb. 2016, *n*=295 U.S. parents of teens who regularly attend youth group.

knowledge of the Bible (65%) and with his or her spiritual maturity (61%). Protestant parents (77%) tend to be more satisfied than Catholic parents (40%) with their youth pastor's Bible knowledge.

When it comes to the teen interaction and operational categories, Protestants are also more prone than Catholics to be very satisfied on "knows how to have fun," and to express the highest level of satisfaction on "keeps kids engaged." Likewise, they tend to be more satisfied than Catholics when it comes to "program planning." Lower income parents are more inclined to be very satisfied with how their youth pastor "helps teens' spiritual maturity" and "keeps kids safe," while the high-income cohort expresses satisfaction that he or she is a "good speaker."

ASSESSING THE CHALLENGES

When youth pastors consider major challenges to the effectiveness of their program, three-quarters agree that teens' busyness tops the list (74%). No other potential obstacle comes close.

Yet parents do not agree. Only one out of nine U.S. parents says their child is "way too busy" (11%). About six in 10 say the balance of activities "is good" (58%), and three in 10 say their teen "needs more to do" (31%).

PARENT PERSPECTIVES ON THEIR TEEN'S ACTIVITY LEVEL
% among U.S. parents of teens

● way too busy   ● balance is good   ● needs more to do

11%
31%
58%

Feb. 2016, n=606 U.S. parents of teens.

It may be that at least some parents are concerned about college admissions in their evaluation of their child's activity level. If this is the case, they are likely biased in favor of more activities over more downtime. Perhaps supporting this thesis, high-income parents (whose children are most likely to attend college) are likelier than others to say their teen "needs more to do."

What do U.S. teens spend their time doing? According to their parents, more than half are involved in sports of some kind (48%) and about two in five are in school band or another musical discipline (37%). One-quarter of teens has a job (19%) or is involved in art, photography or filmmaking (20%), while somewhat fewer are in drama, theater or dance (17%) or an academic club (16%).

Parents whose teen has a job are less likely to say that their child attends youth group weekly or more often, which suggests that working, more than other activities, detracts from youth group

TEEN ACTIVITIES, ACCORDING TO THEIR PARENTS
% "at least once a week" among U.S. parents of teens

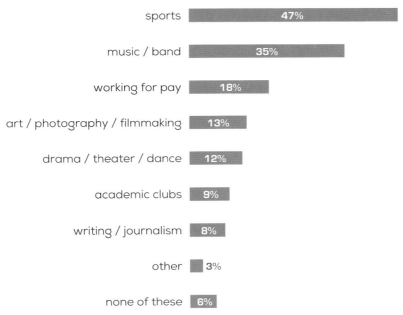

Activity	%
sports	47%
music / band	35%
working for pay	18%
art / photography / filmmaking	13%
drama / theater / dance	12%
academic clubs	9%
writing / journalism	8%
other	3%
none of these	6%

Feb. 2016, *n*=606 U.S. parents of teens.

involvement. Outside of that, there is not a strong negative correlation between activities and youth group attendance. In fact, the opposite is true: Most parents who say their teen does any activity other than "working for pay" tend to report more regular youth group attendance than those who do not engage in extracurricular activities.

Consistent youth-group involvement alongside other commitments may be a credit to the persistence and flexibility of youth pastors; 46 percent of parents feel youth pastors "definitely" accommodate activities around the schedules of teens, and 45 percent say they "sometimes" do.

In the constellation of non-school activities, Christian parents generally consider involvement in youth group to be of equal importance with extracurricular activities (55%), while three in 10 say it is more important (8% much more, 22% somewhat more). In general, higher education levels correlate to a higher value on youth-group involvement.

It's a good bet that youth pastors agree with parents who put a premium on youth group. Yet, in addition to teens' busyness,

DO YOUTH PASTORS ACCOMMODATE TEENS' SCHEDULES?: PARENTS

% among U.S. parents whose teen regularly attends youth group and is involved in at least one other activity

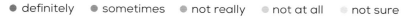
● definitely   ● sometimes   ● not really   ● not at all   ● not sure

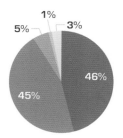

1%
3%
5%
46%
45%

Feb. 2016, *n*=274 U.S. parents whose teen regularly attends youth group and is involved in other activities.

IMPORTANCE OF YOUTH GROUP VS. EXTRACURRICULARS: PARENTS

% among U.S. parents whose teen regularly attends youth group

<---youth group   extracurricular activities--->

| 8% | 22% | 55% | 10% | 5% |

Feb. 2016, n=295 U.S. parents of teens who regularly attend youth group.

these leaders see a host of other challenges to their ministry success—including "lack of interest from parents" (34%) and a "lack of adult volunteers" (29%). One-quarter of youth pastors says the "breakdown of families"—such as absentee parents, divorce or other dysfunctions in the home—is a challenge (24%). These hurdles are all related in some way to adult involvement. So even though parents generally see value in their child's youth-group attendance, youth pastors would like more of them to be directly and meaningfully engaged in the program.

Some youth pastors also feel pressure from a lack of interest among youth (24%), and one in five mentions that not enough teens are taking on leadership roles in the group (20%). This leadership gap may be related to teens' overbooked lives and reluctance on their part to commit at a more demanding level.

Challenges related to financial or material resources—such as a lack of appropriate facilities (12%), church resources (11%) or youth resources (8%)—are mentioned less frequently. A lack of support from church leadership (6%) and a need for quality curricula (4%) fall near the bottom of the list.

Naturally, a lack of appropriate facilities is more often cited as a pain point by youth pastors in smaller churches. In larger congregations, however, leaders are more focused on challenges posed by the breakdown of teens' family structures. White youth pastors are less likely to be worried about a lack of financial resources, but are very concerned about the busyness of teens. Younger youth pastors are more likely to feel impaired by a lack of parental interest in the program.

PARENTS GENERALLY CONSIDER INVOLVEMENT IN YOUTH GROUP TO BE OF EQUAL IMPORTANCE WITH EXTRACURRICULAR ACTIVITIES

THE BIGGEST CHALLENGES FOR YOUTH MINISTRIES IN 2016: YOUTH PASTORS

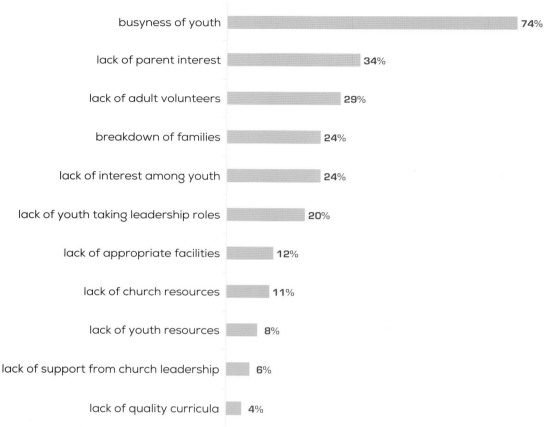

busyness of youth	74%
lack of parent interest	34%
lack of adult volunteers	29%
breakdown of families	24%
lack of interest among youth	24%
lack of youth taking leadership roles	20%
lack of appropriate facilities	12%
lack of church resources	11%
lack of youth resources	8%
lack of support from church leadership	6%
lack of quality curricula	4%

Feb. 2016, *n*=352 U.S. youth pastors; respondents could select up to three options.

Comparing responses of youth pastors in the 2013 study with today's research, Barna found that major ministry challenges haven't dramatically changed in three years. Although kids' busy schedules remain the top concern, slightly fewer leaders mention it today (74%) than in 2013 (86%). Lack of interest from parents (34% vs. 41% 2013) and the breakdown of families (24% vs. 31% 2013) are also a bit less pressing than three years ago. However, the percentage of youth pastors who say they are taxed by a need for adult volunteers has increased; in 2013, about one in five youth pastors expressed that the lack of adult volunteers was the main challenge facing their ministry (22%), compared to about three in 10 today (29%).

The data in Part One reveals that the primary drivers—and hurdles—of a youth program are relational in nature, centered on how ministries connect with parents and teens. In Part Two, we'll discuss the activities and approaches that youth ministries use to steward these connections.

THE PRIMARY DRIVERS—
AND HURDLES—OF A
YOUTH PROGRAM ARE
RELATIONAL

Q&A WITH KARA POWELL

KARA POWELL
Pastor, speaker, writer

Kara Powell, PhD, is the executive director of the Fuller Youth Institute and a faculty member at Fuller Theological Seminary. Named by *Christianity Today* as one of "50 Women to Watch," Kara serves as a youth and family strategist for Orange, and speaks regularly at parenting and leadership conferences. Kara is the author or coauthor of a number of books, including *Growing Young, The Sticky Faith Guide for Your Family, Sticky Faith Curriculum, Can I Ask That?, Deep Justice Journeys, Essential Leadership, Deep Justice in a Broken World, Deep Ministry in a Shallow World* and the *Good Sex Youth Ministry Curriculum.*

www.FullerYouthInstitute.org

Q: Pastors identify a "lack of parent interest" and "lack of adult volunteers" as some of the top challenges to their ministry. Why do you feel it's difficult to capture the focus of parents and adults in their congregations? What are some ways youth ministries can better cultivate and keep their interest?

A: It doesn't surprise me that leaders are disappointed by the lack of parent and volunteer support. When I was serving as a youth pastor, those factors were also among my top three challenges.

Looking back, I struggled to capture the focus of parents and adults *because they were not my focus.* I gave them far too little attention and time. Our church believed the lie that they could outsource the spiritual development of our young people solely to me as the professional youth leader—perhaps because I never told them otherwise.

Now that I'm a parent, I realize I stay better engaged when our youth pastors communicate with me—in advance, and with accurate information. I love that our church has a weekly email to parents and offers annual parent-pastor conferences so we can talk face to face about each of our kids. I also beam when our leaders text, email or call me with a story about one of my kids, or just to let me know they are praying for us. As they dive into our family, it's so much easier for our family to dive into our student ministry.

Q: Many parents say the goal of youth group is to provide a safe space for their child or to be a catalyst for healthy friendships. Why do you think these social concerns are so urgent for parents of teens today?

A: I think parents are often afraid that the hazards of our culture will trip up and derail their kids, so they hope the church will offer their kids some safety. On some levels this is not a bad hope at all; church *should* be a safe place for young people.

But safety can't mean their kid stops growing. It can't mean comfort, and it can't mean their child never falls or fails. Not only is that unrealistic; it's not healthy.

The safety I want our church to offer my kids is the freedom to explore. The freedom to ask hard questions about God and faith. And I long for our youth ministry and the adults pouring into our teenagers to help them choose the right path, to journey with them and to help dust them off when—note I said *when* and not *if*—they stumble.

Our research has shown that struggle and doubt aren't toxic to faith. Silence and lack of trying are.

STRUGGLE AND DOUBT AREN'T TOXIC TO FAITH. SILENCE AND LACK OF TRYING ARE

PART TWO

THE HOW OF YOUTH MINISTRY

Having a vision for youth ministry is one thing; executing an effective youth program is another entirely. Now that we've examined the expressed goals of student ministries, it's helpful to look at the logistics of accomplishing those goals. In short, what do modern youth groups actually *do*?

Part Two covers the practices of youth ministries, as well as the teams that carry them out. What are the methods and curricula employed by youth pastors? How many teens are reached by these efforts? And who are the people behind the scenes making youth ministry happen?

WHO MAKES A YOUTH GROUP?

ON AVERAGE, THE TYPICAL YOUTH MINISTRY INCLUDES

12 adult volunteers (5 of whom are parents of teens in the youth group)

60 teens

1.4 paid youth ministry staff

TRENDS IN YOUTH GROUP ATTENDANCE

69%

TWO-THIRDS OF CHRISTIAN PARENTS SAY THEIR CHILD GOES TO A YOUTH MINISTRY AT LEAST ONCE A WEEK

88% The vast majority of teens attend the same church as their parents

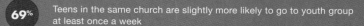
69% Teens in the same church are slightly more likely to go to youth group at least once a week

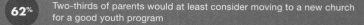
62% Two-thirds of parents would at least consider moving to a new church for a good youth program

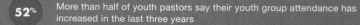
52% More than half of youth pastors say their youth group attendance has increased in the last three years

Parents with higher income are more likely to let their teen choose a church or to change churches for youth program

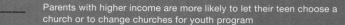
49% Definitely would change churches (vs 15% of others)

48% Definitely would allow their teen to choose (vs 20% of others)

n=352 U.S. youth pastors; n=606 parents of teenagers ages 13–19 (295 parents of teenagers who attend a youth group regularly) | Feb. 2016

3.

MINISTRY PRACTICES

ACTIVITIES

There are some differences in how senior pastors and youth pastors report the regular activities of their youth ministries. But, across the board, they point to plenty of chances for teens to gather, suggesting that youth programs are addressing the social concerns of parents, as well as acting on the ministry's relational goals.

If a teen goes to youth services, there is a pretty good chance they also have an opportunity to attend adult services. More than eight in 10 pastors (87% senior pastors, 84% youth pastors) mention that youth attendance in the main worship service is an activity regularly offered by their youth ministry.

Social activities are a common aspect of youth ministry, as well (85% youth pastors, 84% senior pastors). When the social and spiritual overlap, the result often takes the form of small discipleship or Bible study groups (80% all pastors). This is a key way in which leaders pursue their goal of providing spiritual instruction. However, small groups designated specifically for prayer aren't quite as common; 29 percent of senior pastors and 23 percent of youth pastors list prayer groups as a regular activity.

Youth pastors are more likely than senior pastors to mention offering activities such as large group teaching (71% vs. 49%) and large group worship (48% vs. 30%). However, more than half of all pastors (56% youth pastors, 54% senior pastors) say their church takes teens to youth conferences, which are often

YOUTH PROGRAMS ARE ADDRESSING THE SOCIAL CONCERNS OF PARENTS AND ACTING ON THE MINISTRY'S RELATIONAL GOALS

another opportunity to experience teaching and worship in a large group setting.

While it's clear that youth ministries encourage teens to frequently come together with peers and in groups, valuable one-on-one time with adults is not always an option. One-quarter of pastors (25% senior pastors, 23% youth pastors) say they offer adult-teen mentoring programs.

ACTIVITIES OFFERED BY YOUTH MINISTRY: SENIOR PASTORS & YOUTH PASTORS

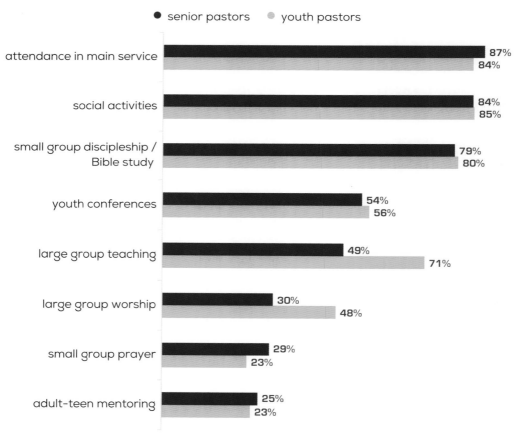

● senior pastors ● youth pastors

attendance in main service — 87% / 84%

social activities — 84% / 85%

small group discipleship / Bible study — 79% / 80%

youth conferences — 54% / 56%

large group teaching — 49% / 71%

large group worship — 30% / 48%

small group prayer — 29% / 23%

adult-teen mentoring — 25% / 23%

Feb. 2016, *n*=381 U.S. senior pastors, *n*=352 U.S. youth pastors.

Senior pastors of large churches—which may have greater resources to facilitate activities that range in size and function—are more likely than leaders of smaller congregations to say they offer large group teaching and worship, small prayer groups and adult-teen mentoring. Youth pastors who are white, young or in a non-mainline church also tend to offer large group activities. On the other hand, urban churches seem to favor intimacy; their senior pastors are more likely than suburban and rural pastors to say they offer small prayer groups and adult-teen mentoring programs, and less likely to list youth attendance in the main service or large group teaching as regular activities.

These are the activities that *pastors* say are available; are parents aware of the same program offerings?

Parents whose teen regularly attends youth group are less likely than pastors to say attendance in the main worship service is a youth group activity: Just over half say this is an aspect of the youth program (45%), about 40 points below pastors' reports. This disparity may reflect how differently pastors and parents think about youth ministry; parents may see teens as more separate from the church body than pastors do.

Six in 10 parents mention social activities (61%), which is in line with their social priorities for the program. Small groups for discipleship (47%) or prayer (45%) are listed by just under half of parents, followed by youth conferences (38%). Large group offerings are recognized in slightly smaller percentages: Worship (33%) and teaching (30%) are activities parents say the youth ministry offers. And when it comes to adult-teen mentoring, parents are in sync with the one-quarter of pastors who say their program offers this activity (28%).

CURRICULUM

Generally, youth pastors use a hybrid of internal and external curricula to conduct their ministry. Seven in 10 report building

ACTIVITIES OFFERED BY YOUTH MINISTRY: PARENTS

% among U.S. Christian parents whose teen regularly attends youth group

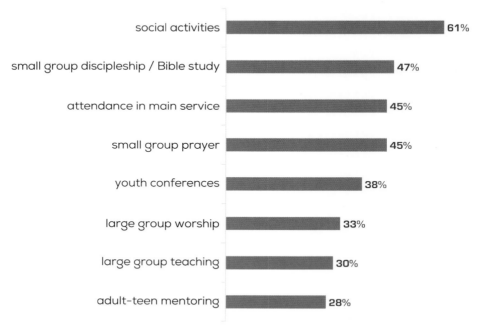

social activities	61%
small group discipleship / Bible study	47%
attendance in main service	45%
small group prayer	45%
youth conferences	38%
large group worship	33%
large group teaching	30%
adult-teen mentoring	28%

Feb. 2016, *n*=295 U.S. parents of teens who regularly attend youth group.

YOUTH PASTORS USE A HYBRID OF INTERNAL AND EXTERNAL CURRICULA TO CONDUCT THEIR MINISTRY

their curriculum resources in-house (71%) and about the same percentage say they purchase teaching tools from outside the church (70%)—meaning there are a sizable number who use both approaches (46%).

Youth pastors over 35 and those in large or rural churches are less likely to purchase curriculum. Also, there is some correlation between the number of paid youth ministry staff and the in-house production of curriculum—that is, the more paid staff, the more likely someone is available to develop custom resources. Seventy-six percent of churches with two or more youth ministry staff members develop their own curriculum, compared to 54 percent of those with no paid staff.

The widespread impulse of youth pastors to create their own curriculum, regardless of whether they also use an outside resources package, may in some cases indicate what might be called "terminal uniqueness"—that is, a view that their ministry context is unlike any other and only they know what is needed in order to be effective. To some extent, this is true. Yet such a mindset may also make it difficult for some leaders to adopt proven best practices or to accept input and insights from ministry veterans. There's not a thing wrong with creating customized resources to meet the needs of kids in a unique context—but it's also good idea to keep learning from the wider community of pastors, mentors and educators.

How are resources, whether internal or external, applied to a youth ministry's regularly offered activities?

Youth pastors report using both in-house materials (68%) and outside resources (75%) for small discipleship and Bible study groups. Elsewhere, youth pastors favor their customized curricula over a purchased version: In-house programs have a lead over outside curricula for large group teaching (65% vs. 50%), social activities (46% vs. 20%), large group worship (39% vs. 22%), youth attendance in main service (29% vs. 9%) and small prayer groups (18% vs. 10%). The only other area in which outside resources are preferred is for youth conferences (30%), where a ministry is less likely to personally handle the teaching and activities. Both forms of curricula prove useful for adult-teen mentoring programs (14%).

RESOURCES USED IN THE YOUTH PROGRAM: YOUTH PASTORS

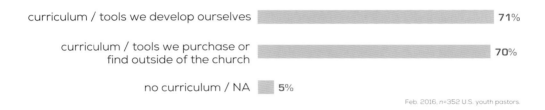

curriculum / tools we develop ourselves — 71%

curriculum / tools we purchase or find outside of the church — 70%

no curriculum / NA — 5%

Feb. 2016, *n*=352 U.S. youth pastors.

RESOURCES PREFERRED FOR MINISTRY ACTIVITIES: YOUTH PASTORS

● tools developed in-house ● purchased curriculum

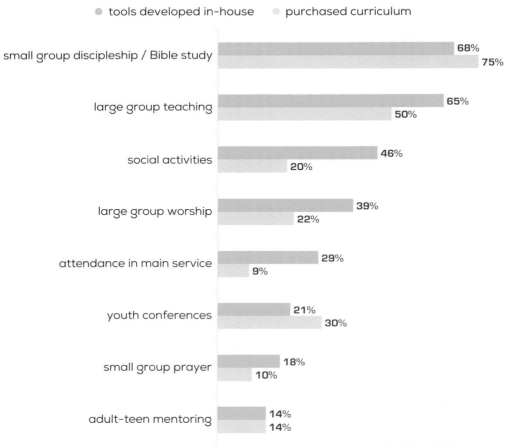

small group discipleship / Bible study 68% / 75%

large group teaching 65% / 50%

social activities 46% / 20%

large group worship 39% / 22%

attendance in main service 29% / 9%

youth conferences 21% / 30%

small group prayer 18% / 10%

adult-teen mentoring 14% / 14%

Feb. 2016, n=352 U.S. youth pastors.

BUDGET

Although every church budget and financial context is—like each youth ministry—unique, the findings reveal broad commonalities among pastors and youth pastors when it comes to operational budgets. According to senior pastors, a majority of churches allocates 10 percent or less of the church budget to youth ministry, with an average of 8 percent. Youth pastors report their churches spend an average of 3 percent of the overall budget on youth ministry, excluding salaries for paid staff positions.

Nearly half of senior pastors (46%) and two in five youth pastors (38%) report that their youth ministry budget increased over the past three years. Similar percentages (43% senior pastors, 41% youth pastors) say there has been no change, while a minority of both senior pastors (11%) and youth pastors (21%) says the youth ministry budget has decreased since three years ago.

YOUTH MINISTRY BUDGET CHANGES, PAST THREE YEARS: SENIOR PASTORS & YOUTH PASTORS

	increased	no change	decreased
senior pastors	46%	43%	11%
youth pastors	38%	41%	21%

Feb. 2016, *n*=381 U.S. senior pastors, *n*=352 U.S. youth pastors.

Senior pastors of medium churches (with 200 to 499 regular attenders) and pastors of urban churches are more likely than others to report a budget increase in the past three years, while those in smaller churches and in majority white churches are less likely to say their youth ministry budget has grown. Youth pastors at large churches tend to report a budget increase. In the Midwest and South, youth pastors are marginally more likely than leaders in other regions to report a decrease.

Tracking the data over time, researchers found that one-third of youth pastors surveyed in 2013 reported an increase (32%) and one-quarter reported a decrease (26%) in their ministry budgets between 2010 and 2013. Today, fewer youth pastors report a decrease (21%), and more say their budget has increased (38%) from 2013 to 2016.

When asked to look ahead to 2019, the vast majority of pastors do not foresee a decrease in the budget for youth ministry. (Later in this report, we take a closer look at the changes pastors predict for the next three years in youth ministry.)

Q&A WITH SHARON GALGAY KETCHAM

Q: Barna findings indicate that social issues are of great concern to the parents of teens in youth ministry. Many feel the goal of youth group is to provide a safe space for their child or to be a catalyst for healthy friendships. Why do you think these social concerns are so urgent for parents of teens today?

On the other hand, senior and youth pastors feel the primary goal of youth ministry is discipleship and spiritual instruction—and they cite the busyness of teens as the number-one challenge of youth ministry. As someone who has studied environments for learning, what are some practical ways that youth pastors can create a culture where spiritual instruction takes hold and has impact?

A: There is a well-known narrative shaping our perception of teenagers. The narrative is as old as the socially created category "teenager" that emerged in the 1900s. We hear it daily in the media, in helicopter parenting and even in our approaches to youth ministry: the idea that teenagers are broken, deficient and in need of help. We problematize teenagers and use significant resources to try and fix them. This narrative evokes fear and, in loving response, parents are desperate to keep them safe. I am not saying we live in a danger-free world; of course there are real dangers. What I am saying is that teenagers are *more* than problems to solve—they have potential as human beings, and surely God sees their potential in Jesus Christ through the work of the Spirit.

Helping teenagers imagine how they might contribute to God's redemptive movement in the world will unveil their potential. When parents, youth pastors and church leaders train their eyes to look beyond the dominant problem narrative, to

SHARON GALGAY KETCHAM
Educator, speaker and author

Sharon Galgay Ketcham is associate professor of theology and Christian ministries at Gordon College in Massachusetts. She earned her PhD in theology and education from Boston College. Sharon's two decades of experience in ministry include serving in full-time ministry, researching, writing, teaching and mentoring. As a practical theologian, she is a scholar for the Church and invites people to reflect theologically on lived Christian faith. She is currently writing a book that examines the community-forming practices essential for a maturing faith among teenagers and adults. Sharon lives in New Hampshire with her husband and two children.

TEENAGERS ARE MORE THAN PROBLEMS TO SOLVE—THEY HAVE POTENTIAL AS HUMAN BEINGS, AND SURELY GOD SEES THEIR POTENTIAL IN JESUS CHRIST

recognize teenage potential and provide a place in the church for teenagers to practice using their gifts, teenagers will find a meaningful purpose in the church. The busyness of teenagers is connected to the longing of adults to help problematized teenagers make it into adulthood. Imagine if we saw teenagers as Christ does: full of potential to join God's purpose.

Q: There are a number of relationships that contribute to effective youth ministry: between senior and youth pastor, between youth pastor and parent, between parent and teen and so on. What are keys to successful communication in these relationships?

A: Relationships are intended to be generative, to produce what is life-giving (see Gen. 1:28). This takes form in mutual giving and receiving. Most relationships, however, have a top-down structure: the old give to the young, the mentor gives to the mentee, the parent gives to the child, the senior pastor gives to the youth pastor. When our expectations of these relationships have a one-way flow, we miss out on what they might generate. We do not need to remove appropriate roles, but our expectations of who gives and who receives in these relationships can stifle the form of communication needed in generative relationships. When we expect the person who is "lower" to give as well as to receive, relationships hold greater life-giving possibilities

Q: How can the church body—both leaders and adult members—better acknowledge and understand the presence of youth in their congregation? What are some practical ways to make their interactions more meaningful, for adults and teens?

A: Mission statements for youth ministries often describe fostering a teenager's relationship with Jesus Christ (with varying theological nuance), but rarely include a focus on a teenager's relationship with the church. This relationship becomes ancillary. A theological question arises: How should we understand a teenager's relationship with the church? Perhaps we do not *believe* this to be a vital relationship, and if this is so, we should not be surprised when teenagers leave the church after high school. Leaders might connect them to Jesus, but what happened to connecting them to the church? Pastors, youth pastors and parents need to reflect theologically on whether fostering a teenager's relationship with the church is vital. If it is, sermons will include relevant illustrations for teenagers, teenagers will contribute in main worship and programming for teenagers will cease to occur simultaneously with the adult service.

PASTORS, YOUTH PASTORS AND PARENTS NEED TO REFLECT THEOLOGICALLY ON WHETHER FOSTERING A TEENAGER'S RELATIONSHIP WITH THE CHURCH IS VITAL

4.

ATTENDANCE

To better grasp the reach and effectiveness of youth ministry practices, it's helpful to look at who is actually attending and involved in youth programs. Teens who attend a youth group seem to be consistent about it; more than two-thirds of Christian parents say their child goes to a youth ministry at least once a week (69%). Roughly one-quarter reports less frequent attendance (23%) and about one in 12 says their teen never attends (8%).

The vast majority of teens attend the same church as their parents (88%). And in fact, they are more likely not to attend church at all (8%) than they are to attend a different church (4%). This corresponds with parent expectations: Three-quarters of churchgoing parents feel it's important for their child to be in the same church (48% "extremely," 30% "very"), while just one in four says it's either "somewhat" important (14%) or "not too / not at all" important (9%). Youth group attendance is high in families who all attend the same church: Two-thirds of these parents say their teen goes to youth group at least once a week (69%).

Even so, a majority of parents would be open to their teen exploring other options. Nearly half would "probably" allow their teen to attend elsewhere (40%), and 26 percent "definitely" would allow it. Likewise, if a youth program in another church were appealing to their teen, nearly two-thirds of parents would switch churches for it (38% "probably," 24% "definitely"). The bottom line for most parents is for their child to enjoy their church youth group: 78 percent say this is at least "very important." So, while parents prefer the ideal scenario of attending the church of their

MORE THAN TWO-THIRDS OF CHRISTIAN PARENTS SAY THEIR CHILD GOES TO A YOUTH MINISTRY AT LEAST ONCE A WEEK

FREQUENCY OF TEEN ATTENDANCE AT YOUTH GROUP: PARENTS

% among U.S. Christian parents of teens

● once a week   ● less frequent   ● not at all

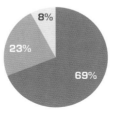

Feb. 2016, *n*=438 U.S. self-identified Christian parents of teens.

LOCATION OF TEEN ATTENDANCE AT YOUTH GROUP: PARENTS

% among U.S. Christian parents of teens

● same church as parents   ● different church than parents   ● not at all

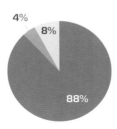

Feb. 2016, *n*=438 U.S. self-identified Christian parents of teens.

choice alongside their teen, they ultimately will do what they can to see their child attend a ministry that meets their needs, wherever it may be.

Parents with higher incomes are especially adaptable in this regard. Although they are more likely than other parents to appreciate their child's attendance at the same church, they are also

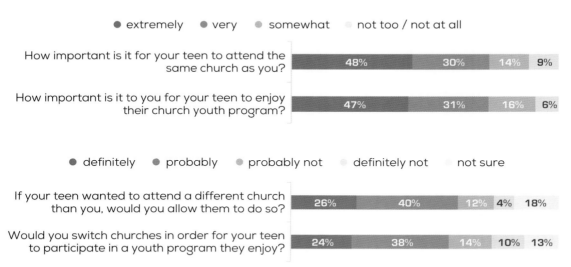

TEENS' CHURCH ATTENDANCE & ENJOYMENT OF YOUTH GROUP: PARENTS

% among U.S. Christian parents of teens

● extremely ● very ● somewhat ○ not too / not at all

How important is it for your teen to attend the same church as you?
48% | 30% | 14% | 9%

How important is it to you for your teen to enjoy their church youth program?
47% | 31% | 16% | 6%

● definitely ● probably ● probably not ○ definitely not ○ not sure

If your teen wanted to attend a different church than you, would you allow them to do so?
26% | 40% | 12% | 4% | 18%

Would you switch churches in order for your teen to participate in a youth program they enjoy?
24% | 38% | 14% | 10% | 13%

Feb. 2016, n=438 U.S. self-identified Christian parents of teens.

62% OF PARENTS SAY THEY WOULD SWITCH CHURCHES IN ORDER FOR THEIR TEEN TO PARTICIPATE IN A YOUTH PROGRAM THEY ENJOY

more likely to allow their child to attend elsewhere and to follow them to a church with a better youth ministry. Half say they would switch (49%), compared to about one in five middle-income parents (22%) and one in 11 lower income families (9%).

Very few parents in this study say their teen actively attends another church, so it's difficult for researchers to draw broad conclusions as to the reasons some teens break out on their own. But there are notable responses in this small sample. The most common reason their teen attends another church, according to parents, is "My teen prefers a youth program at another church." But there are also social drivers at work, such as "There are not many kids my teenager's age at my church" and "My teen's friends go to another church." For some it's just a matter of diverging preferences: "I prefer a different church than the one my teen prefers" or "My teen does not like the youth program at my church." A few teens like the Young Life program or, for a few, the parent does not attend church regularly. Which poses the question: What do these teens most like about their other church? Parents indicate a preference for the worship style (71%), social activities (71%), friends who go to the church (59%) or the pastor of the youth ministry (59%). Smaller percentages also say the general feel (45%) or the teaching (45%) play a part.

To get a more complete picture of youth group attendance, researchers turned to estimates among church leaders. Based on pastors' responses, the average (median) youth group reaches 30 teens a week. Attendance is highly correlated with church size, as one might expect: Each week, there is an average of 20 teens in small churches, 48 in medium churches and 136 in large churches, according to youth pastors. Senior pastors report similar weekly estimates: 20 teens in small churches, 35 in medium churches and 136 in large churches on average.

Most pastors and youth pastors are upbeat about attendance growth. Most church leaders say their youth group has grown over the past three years; half of senior pastors (51%) and youth pastors (52%) report an attendance increase since 2013. About one-quarter of ministers estimate the youth ministry numbers have either held steady (25% senior pastors, 22% youth pastors) or seen a decrease (24% senior pastors, 26% youth pastors).

MOST CHURCH LEADERS SAY THEIR YOUTH GROUP HAS GROWN OVER THE PAST THREE YEARS

YOUTH GROUP ATTENDANCE CHANGES, PAST THREE YEARS: SENIOR PASTORS & YOUTH PASTORS

	increased	no change	decreased
senior pastors	51%	25%	24%
youth pastors	52%	22%	26%

Feb. 2016, *n*=381 U.S. senior pastors, *n*=352 U.S. youth pastors.

5.

STAFFING & VOLUNTEERS

As we examined in the section on ministry strengths, a majority of churches trend more strongly toward discipleship than toward outreach. However, churches with at least one paid youth ministry staff tend to be more focused on reaching teens than churches with no ministry staff. This suggests that having a paid employee could contribute to a sense of mission or urgency when it comes to reaching teens outside the church. Most churches have one youth ministry staff member, according to senior pastors. More than half have one paid staff member dedicated to youth (55%) and 17 percent have two or more; the remaining 28 percent do not have a paid staff member. The number of paid staff is weakly correlated with youth group size, with the largest groups having an average of two paid staff members.

Most churches with paid, designated youth ministry staff plan to continue with this approach. Eight out of 10 senior pastors say they do not anticipate replacing paid staff with a volunteer in the next year (81%). However, leaders of urban churches are twice as likely as the average to say yes, they plan to replace paid youth ministry staff with a volunteer (21% vs. 6% all pastors). On the other hand, white senior leaders are much more likely to say they do *not* anticipate replacing a youth pastor with a volunteer (87% vs. 55% all others).

Churches without a paid youth minister are not always content with their current strategy. Senior leaders of these congregations are more likely to say they expect to increase staffing (41% vs. 28% churches with paid youth staff). Likewise, a majority of

CHURCHES WITH AT LEAST ONE PAID YOUTH MINISTRY STAFF MEMBER TEND TO BE MORE FOCUSED ON REACHING TEENS THAN CHURCHES WITH NO MINISTRY STAFF

youth pastors in rural churches expects their staffing to increase somewhat in the next three years (54%).

The average youth leader spends about half a decade—five-and-a-half years—as youth leader in their church. Most go through more than one position during their tenure in youth ministry; on average, youth leaders hold between two and three separate roles in youth ministry and spend just over three years in one position.

Who are today's youth pastors? The data sketch a general profile: young, educated, married and male.

The majority of youth pastors—four out of five—are male (81%). In non-mainline churches, an overwhelming 90 percent of youth pastors are men, while there is a smaller gender gap in mainline churches: Among these congregations, two out of five youth pastors are female (42%). Like non-mainline youth groups, larger churches have a higher proportion of male youth ministers.

Youth pastors are typically married (84%); just 16 percent have either never been or are no longer married. Three out of five have children under 18 years old in their household (60%).

Most youth pastors in this study are under the age of 40. The largest age group is between 30 and 39 years old (49%), followed by the 26–29 (18%) and 40–49 (16%) age groups. Parents tend to list their youth pastor as slightly older than their actual age (and also perceive a slightly higher proportion of female youth pastors than is actually the case).

Generally, youth pastors are an educated group, many with focused ministry training. Nearly half are college graduates (47%). One-third attended seminary (34%), and 7 percent have "some" seminary training. Those with only some college (8%), a high school education (2%) or trade school training (2%) are in the minority. This reflects the high regard senior pastors have for specific youth ministry training. The majority of senior leaders say this kind of education is important (24% "extremely," 43% "very") and just 5 percent say it is either not that important or not at all important. Urban pastors and pastors of large churches

WHO ARE TODAY'S YOUTH PASTORS? YOUNG, EDUCATED, MARRIED AND MALE generally rate specific training more highly than others, and white pastors are more likely to list it as "extremely important."

Eight in 10 youth ministers hold a full-time position at their current church (49%). In addition to full-time youth leadership, three in 10 are also in charge of another ministry area (30%).

A plurality moves on within three years: 39 percent of youth pastors in this study are in their first three years of ministry in their congregation. The numbers significantly taper off after 10 years, with only 12 percent reporting they have been in ministry at their church for more than a decade.

Beyond paid youth leaders, volunteers play a significant and sometimes lead role in youth groups. And, as we've seen, a lack of adult volunteers and parent interest is a pivotal concern for many ministry leaders. Overall, youth groups have an average of 12 adults who volunteer on a regular basis, with an average of seven who are not parents of students. The average number of

YEARS IN YOUTH MINISTRY AT CURRENT CHURCH: YOUTH PASTORS

number of years, among U.S. youth pastors

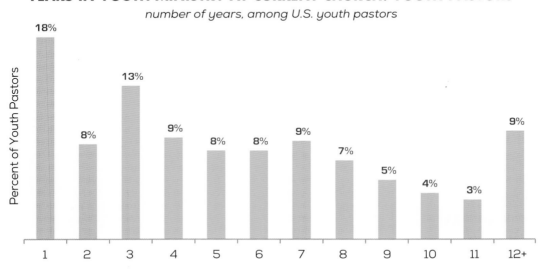

Feb. 2016, *n*=352 U.S. youth pastors.

volunteers is correlated with both youth group size and church size. Of parents whose teens attend a youth group consistently, a plurality reports volunteering regularly (42%). One-third occasionally volunteers (33%) and one-quarter reports they do not volunteer (25%).

One important function of youth group volunteers is to help youth volunteer themselves in acts of service to their church, community and other places. Part Three focuses on how youth ministries incorporate service opportunities and the impact of these endeavors.

THEN AND NOW: TRACKING CHANGE IN YOUTH MINISTRY

IN 2013, YOUTH PASTORS SAID THEY LOOKED FORWARD TO ...

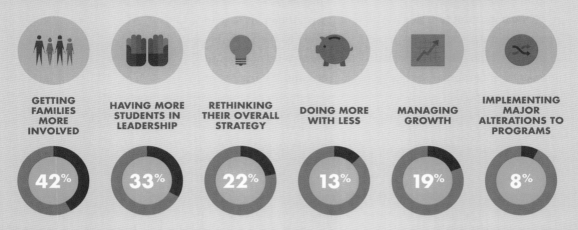

GETTING FAMILIES MORE INVOLVED	HAVING MORE STUDENTS IN LEADERSHIP	RETHINKING THEIR OVERALL STRATEGY	DOING MORE WITH LESS	MANAGING GROWTH	IMPLEMENTING MAJOR ALTERATIONS TO PROGRAMS
42%	33%	22%	13%	19%	8%

EXPECTATIONS VS. REALITY

In 2013, youth pastors were asked if they expected to grow, decline or hold steady in key aspects of their program. Then, in 2016, youth pastors were encouraged to assess the changes that had occurred over the past three years. Side-by-side, these responses offer a helpful comparison between the vision and performance of youth ministry. Occasionally, hopes proved to be a little too high—such as when three-quarters of youth pastors in 2013 predicted attendance growth. But for the most part, leaders seem to have good instincts about the paths of their programs.

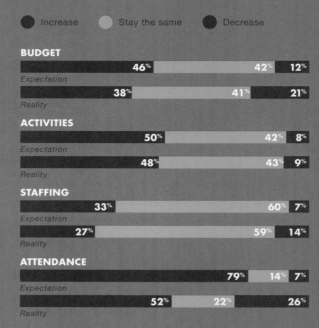

● Increase ● Stay the same ● Decrease

BUDGET
Expectation: 46% / 42% / 12%
Reality: 38% / 41% / 21%

ACTIVITIES
Expectation: 50% / 42% / 8%
Reality: 48% / 43% / 9%

STAFFING
Expectation: 33% / 60% / 7%
Reality: 27% / 59% / 14%

ATTENDANCE
Expectation: 79% / 14% / 7%
Reality: 52% / 22% / 26%

n=463 youth pastors | Oct. 2013
n=352 youth pastors | Feb. 2016

TRACKING CHANGES:
THE NEXT THREE YEARS

A significant goal of this research is to track expectations of leaders over time to better understand the successes and growing pains of youth groups. As the data visualization on the previous pages shows, reality doesn't always unfold according to pastors' expectations: In 2016, leaders discovered that the changes they predicted in 2013 for the coming three years didn't pan out exactly to plan.

Which is okay! Spot-on future-casting isn't the point. Rather, leaders' predictions can serve as a helpful proxy for their hopes and prayers for their youth ministry. So here, for the record, are pastors' 2016 predictions for the *next* three years. Researchers hope to check back with them again in 2019 to find out how leaders' overall optimism for the near future helped them engage in effective ministry.

LEADERS' PREDICTIONS CAN SERVE AS A HELPFUL PROXY FOR THEIR HOPES AND PRAYERS

MAJOR CHANGES
Nearly three in 10 youth pastors predict that, in three years, they will have more families involved in their youth group (28%). About one-quarter expects more student leaders (23%), and one in five plans to rethink their overall strategy (22%). Other shifts include managing growth (14%), implementing major changes to programs (7%) and doing more with less (4%). These responses show confidence despite some of the challenges pastors name, such as a lack of adult volunteers, parent interest or youth in leadership roles.

ATTENDANCE
About seven in 10 among both senior pastors (74%) and youth pastors (71%) anticipate an increase in youth attendance. Seventeen percent of both groups of leaders predict there will be no change. About one in 10 (11% youth pastors, 9% senior pastors) says their attendance will likely decrease over the next few years.

Young youth pastors, youth ministers in large churches, leaders in the Northeast and those in non-mainline churches are more likely to expect significant increases in youth group attendance. Black youth pastors and female leaders, however, are more pessimistic overall about youth group growth. When it comes to senior pastors, those in majority black churches and in churches with more than 500 regular attenders are much more assured about the growth of their ministry programs.

ACTIVITIES

Although senior pastors are more enthusiastic, both senior pastors (62%) and youth pastors (46%) are likely to predict that the number of youth group activities will increase. A greater percentage of youth pastors (44% vs. 34% senior pastors) predict no change to current offerings. Ten percent of youth pastors think activities may decrease, while just a small proportion of senior pastors feel this way (3%).

Youth pastors who are non-white, or are in the West or Northeast, are more likely to predict they will offer more activities. Among senior pastors, those in urban churches are more likely to expect some increase, but 10 percent of those in suburban churches hope for "significant growth" in their activities, larger than any other group.

BUDGET

A majority of senior pastors (65%) and a plurality of youth leaders (47%) plan on a budget increase for the youth ministry over the next three years. Two out of five youth pastors (41%) assume no change, while three in 10 senior pastors make this prediction (29%). Twelve percent of youth pastors and 5 percent of senior pastors say their youth ministry will experience budget cuts by 2019.

Younger youth ministers and those in the West are more likely to expect a significant increase in budget, even as leaders in churches with no full-time youth ministry staff are much more likely to anticipate a significant decrease. Senior pastors in large

BOTH SENIOR PASTORS
AND YOUTH PASTORS
PREDICT THE NUMBER
OF YOUTH GROUP
ACTIVITIES WILL INCREASE

and urban churches especially expect an expanded budget in the next three years.

STAFFING

Staffing is one area in which a majority of both senior and youth pastors do not expect growth. More than half say their youth ministry staff will remain the same (59% senior pastors, 52% youth pastors). If they don't expect to hold steady staffing levels, most other senior (38%) and youth pastors (37%) foresee an increase in employees, while smaller percentages are preparing for their team to diminish (3% senior pastors, 11% youth pastors).

A majority of youth pastors in rural areas expects their staffing to increase somewhat. Senior pastors in churches that do not have a paid youth minister (41%) are more likely to say they expect to add to their youth ministry staff than churches that already have a dedicated youth minister (28%).

STAFFING IS ONE AREA IN WHICH A MAJORITY OF BOTH SENIOR AND YOUTH PASTORS DO NOT EXPECT GROWTH

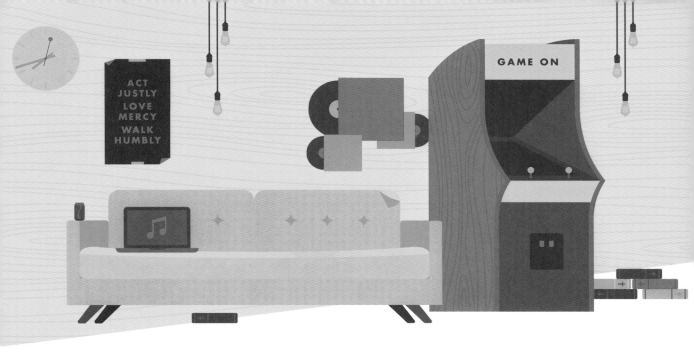

PART THREE

SERVICE & YOUTH MINISTRY

From car washes and mission trips to Bible donations and neighborhood cleanups, service projects have become almost synonymous with the youth group experience. They make up a major part of the public picture of youth ministry, and have become almost a rite of passage for the Christian adolescent.

But serving is more than a milestone of maturity. It's a unique opportunity for God's people to pursue justice and express compassion, while instilling in teens a habit of service that will follow them into adulthood.

Nine out of 10 youth pastors report that their ministry engages in service: 88 percent have participated in a project or trip of some kind. Part Three explores the multitude of forms that service can take, the reasons pastors and parents find serving valuable and the lasting impact it may have on the community—and the teens—involved.

THE MYTH OF THE LAZY TEEN

There might not be too much to the stereotypical narratives of self-absorbed or "slacktivist" teens. Barna found today's youth are actively engaged in service and volunteer projects—and youth ministry is a primary channel through which they serve. Here are a few themes of the altruistic habits of teens, as reported by their parents.

TEENS ARE ACTIVE VOLUNTEERS

According to their parents, a majority of teens (65%) are fairly active when it comes to volunteering at least once every few months.

20%	AT LEAST ONCE A WEEK
23%	AT LEAST ONCE EVERY MONTH
22%	ONCE EVERY FEW MONTHS
35%	LESS OFTEN

TEEN VOLUNTEERING FOCUSES ON CHURCH SERVICE & POVERTY ALLEVIATION

The most common forms of service for teens are those associated with their church or youth group. But there are some other key areas in which teens express compassion and give of their time.

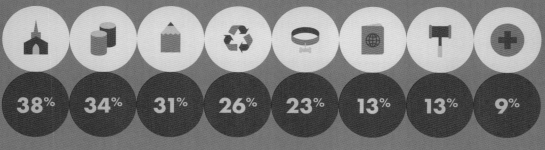

Church / ministry	Feeding the hungry / Helping the homeless	Educational	Environmental / Cleanup	Animal	Service trips	Social or political advocacy	Medical or healthcare
38%	34%	31%	26%	23%	13%	13%	9%

THE CHURCH IS CENTRAL TO TEEN VOLUNTEERING EFFORTS

When parents of teens who attend youth group regularly are asked specifically whether their teen has participated in a service project with a church, six in 10 (58%) say yes.

THE PRIMARY WAYS TEENS ENGAGE IN SERVICE THROUGH THEIR CHURCH

55% DAYS OF SERVICE AT CHURCH

49% DAYS OF SERVICE IN THEIR TOWN

44% A SERVICE COMMITMENT ON A REGULAR BASIS

35% SERVICE AT A DESTINATION THAT COULD BE REACHED IN A DAY'S DRIVE

19% SERVICE AT A DESTINATION IN THE U.S. THAT IS FARTHER THAN A DAY'S DRIVE

10% A MISSION TRIP OUTSIDE THE U.S.

THE GOALS OF SERVICE ARE TO LOVE AND SERVE OTHERS

 73% **56%**

THREE-QUARTERS OF YOUTH PASTORS SAY LOVING AND SERVING OTHERS IS THE PRIMARY GOAL OF YOUTH MISSION TRIPS ... MORE THAN HALF OF PARENTS AGREE

OTHER GOALS OF MISSION TRIPS

● Youth Pastors   ◗ Parents

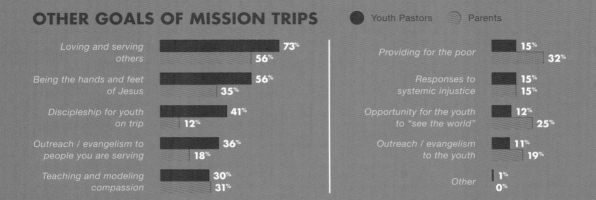

	Youth Pastors	Parents
Loving and serving others	73%	56%
Being the hands and feet of Jesus	56%	35%
Discipleship for youth on trip	41%	12%
Outreach / evangelism to people you are serving	36%	18%
Teaching and modeling compassion	30%	31%
Providing for the poor	15%	32%
Responses to systemic injustice	15%	15%
Opportunity for the youth to "see the world"	12%	25%
Outreach / evangelism to the youth	11%	19%
Other	1%	0%

n=606 parents of teenagers ages 13–19 (295 parents of teenagers who attend a youth group regularly) | n=352 youth pastors | Feb. 2016

6.

GOALS OF SERVING

A MAJORITY OF YOUTH
PASTORS SAYS THE GOAL
OF SERVING IS TO LOVE
AND SERVE OTHERS OR
TO BE THE HANDS AND
FEET OF JESUS

LEADER GOALS

Youth pastors were presented with a list of potential motivations for mission and asked to select up to three that describe their goals for such projects. The most popular responses are linked to a broader sense of calling. Three-quarters choose "loving and serving others" (73%), and more than half choose "being the hands and feet of Jesus" (56%).

Four in 10 prioritize how service can benefit teens, not just the people they are serving: 41 percent say "discipleship for youth on a trip" is a main goal.

Just behind this reason is "outreach to people and organizations" (36%). (Among those who select this option, three in five believe it is important that outreach should involve explicitly sharing the gospel through evangelism and compassion.) Thirty percent think "teaching and modeling compassion" is a primary reason for service.

Less common goals of service include responding to systemic injustice (15%), providing for the poor (15%), allowing teens to see the world (12%) and conducting outreach and evangelism for youth (11%). Youth pastors in urban churches (25%) tend to be more interested in responding to systemic injustice than their colleagues in suburban (15%), small town (8%) and rural churches (7%).

Female youth leaders are more connected to some of the abstract goals like loving and serving others or representing the hands and feet of Christ, while male youth leaders are more likely to list outreach and evangelism. Youth pastors in mainline

THE GOAL OF COMMUNITY SERVICE & MISSION TRIPS: YOUTH PASTORS

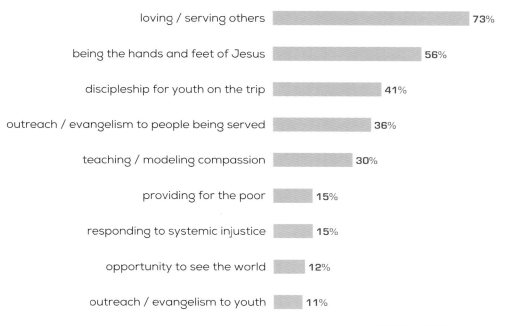

loving / serving others	73%
being the hands and feet of Jesus	56%
discipleship for youth on the trip	41%
outreach / evangelism to people being served	36%
teaching / modeling compassion	30%
providing for the poor	15%
responding to systemic injustice	15%
opportunity to see the world	12%
outreach / evangelism to youth	11%

Feb. 2016, *n*=352 U.S. youth pastors.

churches are also more likely to be motivated by showing love and service rather than by outreach and evangelism.

Black leaders demonstrate a deeper concern for providing for the poor and are less likely to list loving and serving others as a main goal. Youth pastors in the Midwest are slightly more likely to be driven by addressing systemic injustice, but also connect with the metaphor of being Jesus' hands and feet.

Researchers also asked youth pastors to rate the appeal of a mission trip based on potential outcomes in their ministry. Topping the list of "very appealing" outcomes are "students experience growth in their faith development" (82%), closely followed by "students meet real needs and make a difference" (77%).

Roughly two-thirds say "students can serve alongside a community" (63%) and "students build relationships with those in a community" (62%) are very appealing outcomes.

APPEAL OF MISSION TRIPS BASED ON POTENTIAL OUTCOMES: YOUTH PASTORS

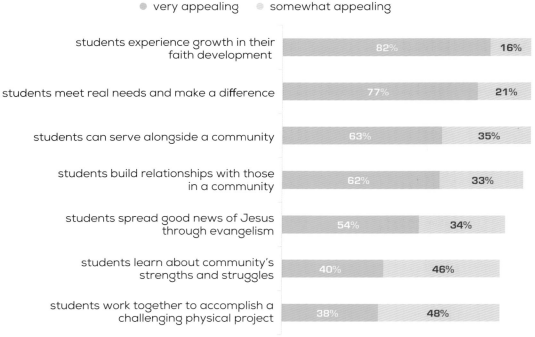

● very appealing   ● somewhat appealing

	very appealing	somewhat appealing
students experience growth in their faith development	82%	16%
students meet real needs and make a difference	77%	21%
students can serve alongside a community	63%	35%
students build relationships with those in a community	62%	33%
students spread good news of Jesus through evangelism	54%	34%
students learn about community's strengths and struggles	40%	46%
students work together to accomplish a challenging physical project	38%	48%

Feb. 2016, *n*=352 U.S. youth pastors.

PARENT GOALS

Parents see volunteering as an important practice—not only for their teen, but also for themselves. There are a number of reasons that parents say they personally volunteer: to help people in need (76%), help communities or organizations they feel drawn toward (53%), to set a good example for their teen (46%) and to grow as a person (43%). So it makes sense that a large majority of parents—80 percent—find it to be "somewhat" or "very" important that their child participate in community service as well.

What are the specific benefits that parents see in their teen's efforts? They believe it's a way to show young people how to give back from what they have received (48%) or to see and have experiences with someone who is different (45%). More than one-third says it helps kids learn to connect to other people (42%), to be well rounded (36%) or to be empathetic (37%). Some simply see it as a healthy social activity (28%) or an opportunity for a teen to build up their resume or college application (18%). Maybe, as a minority of parents hope, their teen might just enjoy doing it (15%).

EIGHT OUT OF 10 PARENTS SAY IT'S IMPORTANT THAT THEIR CHILD PARTICIPATES IN COMMUNITY SERVICE

THE GOALS OF COMMUNITY SERVICE & MISSION TRIPS: PARENTS

% among U.S. parents whose teen regularly attends youth group

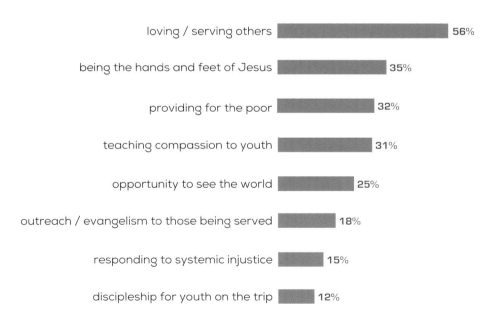

loving / serving others	56%
being the hands and feet of Jesus	35%
providing for the poor	32%
teaching compassion to youth	31%
opportunity to see the world	25%
outreach / evangelism to those being served	18%
responding to systemic injustice	15%
discipleship for youth on the trip	12%

Feb. 2016, n=295 U.S. parents of teens who regularly attend youth group.

Like youth pastors, when considering the goals of community service in the context of youth ministry, parents are drawn to more poetic, aspirational descriptions. More than half select "loving and serving others" (56%) and 35 percent pick "being the hands and feet of Jesus."

Understandably, when it comes to service, parents also think about how it might shape their teen into a better person. One-third of parents are hopeful that participation might stir up a spirit of altruism in their child, saying service is important to "teach compassion to the youth" (31%); a similar proportion says "providing for the poor" is a valuable outcome (32%).

One-quarter of parents says an "opportunity to see the world" is a goal for their teen's service (25%), while about one in six point to "outreach and evangelism to the people being served" (18%). Twelve percent say service is a chance for their teen to be discipled.

Just 15 percent of parents see youth ministry service as a response to systemic injustice. However, parents with lower incomes are more likely to place importance on this goal. They are also more prone to list teaching and modeling compassion to youth, loving and serving others and being the hands and feet of Jesus. Parents with higher incomes are more invested in a service project's ability to disciple the youth on the trip, as well as to provide for the poor.

7.

SERVICE PRACTICES

Nine out of 10 youth pastors say their youth group has engaged in some type of service project within the past two years (88%). Let's take a look at the details.

TYPES OF SERVICE

The majority of service events are conducted within a church's local community. Most commonly, a project takes the form of a day of giving back to the town or city; nearly eight in 10 youth pastors report such an event (78%). Sixty-nine percent have gone to serve at another nearby destination that is within a day's drive. About three out of five say their youth ministry has hosted a day of service at the church itself (58%). According to this study, mainline youth groups are more likely to engage in days of service than groups in non-mainline churches.

Mission trips occur less frequently, which is reasonable, given the planning, funding and travel required to effectively serve in this way. Unsurprisingly, churches with no paid youth ministry staff are not as likely as those with a paid pastor to go on a long-distance mission trip. Still, a significant percentage of all youth pastors report having organized a mission trip of some kind. More than one-quarter have done so to a location within the U.S. farther than a day's drive from the church (27%). Thirty percent have ventured to serve outside of the U.S.

Location, church size and ethnicity each seem to correlate to a different approach to mission trips. Suburban youth ministers

TYPE OF SERVICE PROJECTS: YOUTH PASTORS

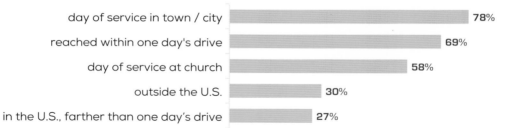

day of service in town / city	78%
reached within one day's drive	69%
day of service at church	58%
outside the U.S.	30%
in the U.S., farther than one day's drive	27%

Feb. 2016, n=309 U.S. youth pastors whose groups do service projects.

are more likely than others to conduct them, and large churches are more likely than smaller congregations to serve outside the U.S. White youth ministers are also more likely than black or Hispanic pastors to take their group on a mission trip.

The length of a mission trip can vary. Seven in 10 youth pastors have led a trip within the past two years that lasted one week (71%), and a similar percentage led a one-day trip (68%). Forty percent have gone on a trip for two or three days, and one in five have stayed longer than a week (20%). Medium churches are more likely than their counterparts to send their youth group on a mission trip lasting one week or longer. Male youth leaders are more likely to have gone on mission trips exceeding one week (23%); just 9 percent of female youth pastors report having done so.

NUMBER OF SERVICE TRIPS: YOUTH PASTORS

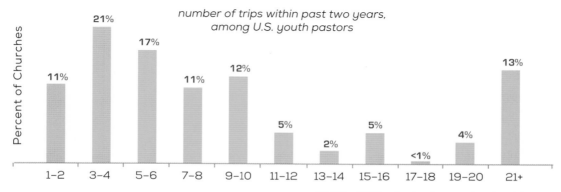

number of trips within past two years, among U.S. youth pastors

Percent of Churches

1–2	3–4	5–6	7–8	9–10	11–12	13–14	15–16	17–18	19–20	21+
11%	21%	17%	11%	12%	5%	2%	5%	<1%	4%	13%

Feb. 2016, n=309 U.S. youth pastors whose groups do service projects.

YOUTH PARTICIPATION

As previously noted, parents think it's important for their child to give of their time and effort to meaningful causes. Outside of the local church, teens may take on various types of volunteering: feeding the hungry (34%), education (31%), environmental issues / cleanup (26%), animals (23%), service trips (13%), social or political advocacy (13%) and medical / healthcare issues (9%). There is a strong correlation between income level and service trips, as well as medical volunteering. Parents of a higher education level are more likely to say their child helps feed the hungry. Non-white parents are particularly drawn toward educational needs.

PARENTS THINK IT'S IMPORTANT FOR THEIR CHILD TO GIVE OF THEIR TIME AND EFFORT TO MEANINGFUL CAUSES

AREAS OF TEEN VOLUNTEERING: PARENTS
% among U.S. parents of teens

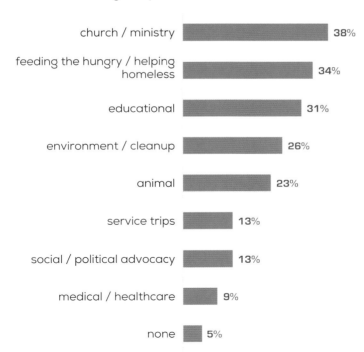

church / ministry	38%
feeding the hungry / helping homeless	34%
educational	31%
environment / cleanup	26%
animal	23%
service trips	13%
social / political advocacy	13%
medical / healthcare	9%
none	5%

Feb. 2016, *n*=606 U.S. parents of teens.

Church-related ministry projects, however, are the top choice for teen volunteering. Overall, 38 percent of parents say their teen serves in this respect at least once a year. Of parents whose teens attend church regularly, 61 percent say their child has participated in a ministry service project. A majority of these indicates it was a day of service at the church (55%), but a similarly popular option is a day of service in their town (49%). More than one-third says their teen has served at a destination within in one day's drive (35%) or has made a commitment to serve on regular basis (44%). One in five has gone on a mission trip to a destination in the U.S. farther than one day's drive (19%), while one in 10 has gone outside of the U.S. (10%).

Teens with wealthier and more highly educated parents, and teens who attend the same church as their parents, are more

CHURCH-RELATED MINISTRY PROJECTS ARE THE TOP CHOICE FOR TEEN VOLUNTEERING

TYPE OF CHURCH SERVICE PROJECTS: PARENTS

% among U.S. parents whose teen participated in a church service project

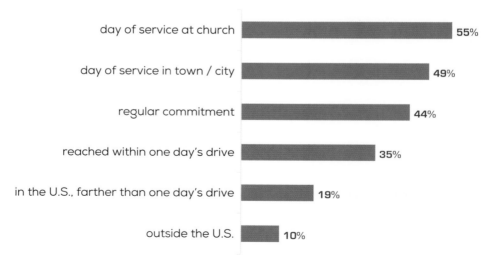

day of service at church	55%
day of service in town / city	49%
regular commitment	44%
reached within one day's drive	35%
in the U.S., farther than one day's drive	19%
outside the U.S.	10%

Feb. 2016, n=179 U.S. parents of teens who participated in a church service project.

likely to participate in service projects. Given the cost of sending a teen on a mission trip, children of lower-income parents tend to serve close to home; these youth are more likely to participate through designated days of service at their church. Higher income parents, however, are more likely to say their teen has participated in a trip to a destination in the U.S. beyond one day's travel.

Although parents paint a compelling picture of youth volunteering habits, one-third also says their teen engages in service less often than every few months (35%). About one-quarter finds a way to give back once every few months (22%) or at least once a month (23%). About one in five serves consistently, at least once a week (20%).

The opportunity to volunteer seems to be somewhat of a socioeconomic privilege. Across the board, frequency of service is strongly correlated with household income. A majority of high-income parents says their teen volunteers at least once a week (36%) or once a month (27%). And though some parents of both middle and lower incomes report that their teen frequently volunteers, the most common response among these two groups is "less often" than every few months (31% middle, 44% lower income).

NEARLY ALL PARENTS FEEL THE SERVICE ACTIVITIES THEIR TEEN PARTICIPATES IN WILL HAVE A LASTING IMPACT

PREPARATION & FOLLOW-UP

Nearly all parents feel the service activities their teen participates in will "definitely" (80%) or "probably" (17%) have a lasting impact. Three percent are not confident in its long-term benefits.

Pre-mission trip, most youth leaders strategically lay the groundwork for the experience—and parents are largely satisfied with the preparation their child received. About two-thirds say their child's preparation was "definitely" adequate (68%), and another 29 percent say it was "somewhat" adequate.

As with pre-trip preparation, parents are generally satisfied with leaders' follow-up efforts and feel their teen is adequately debriefed following a mission trip. More than half say this is "definitely" the case (56%), and 42 percent say "somewhat."

When it comes to post-trip plans, youth pastors understand the impact of a service activity doesn't end when the project closes or the return flight lands. Half say it is "very important" and one-third it's "extremely important" that youth ministries follow up after a service project or trip. Another 18 percent call follow-up "somewhat important" and just 1 percent don't see it as vital.

Follow-up is usually verbal, with the goal of helping teens process the happenings of the service project or trip, as well as to share it with the rest of the group or the whole congregation. The most popular type of follow-up activity is making time for youth to talk about their service experience with other students or the church body (83%). Three-quarters of youth pastors remind students about the continued importance of serving in their everyday life (75%). Two-thirds discuss the trip soon after at a social activity (66%); 45 percent host such an event a few months after the trip. Sixty-three percent encourage prayer for those who have been impacted by the trip, and more than half prepare a lesson or discussion on service (54%).

Other more practical forms of follow-up include finding new or different ways to serve locally (49%), challenging teens to apply what they learned on a trip (48%) and researching more about the needs of the local community (31%).

THE MOST POPULAR TYPE OF FOLLOW-UP ACTIVITY IS MAKING TIME FOR YOUTH TO TALK ABOUT THEIR SERVICE EXPERIENCE WITH OTHER STUDENTS OR THE CHURCH BODY

Q&A WITH DANIEL WHITE HODGE

Q: As someone who focuses on theological and academic study of topics such as film, media and hip-hop, what are some fruitful ways that youth ministries can model engagement with culture and entertainment? How can youth ministries be a companion (to both the home and the school) in terms of helping teens think critically about what they read / watch / listen to?

A: I have found that engagement with this generation of young people, those under 19 years of age, looks more like *being present* than *doing*. Many ethnic-minority youth from a hip-hop context want you to be there, listen, question and grow with them, rather than participate in a full-on program.

One example of how to effectively contextualize a youth ministry for a generation of young people in a certain area comes from Phil Jackson, who runs the nation's premier hip-hop church (The House Church) in Chicago. He built the ministry around the foundational elements of hip-hop culture (breaking, graffiti art, emceeing and DJing). From there, volunteers and paid staff live with and engage youth, with hip-hop as the central premise and ethos of the ministry. The main thing to take away, at least from my research, is to be present and engaged with the young person. Things will come up, and from that, you can walk with them as they develop into adults. Hip-hop, film, music and art are all spaces to engage with the gospel.

I have also found that part of that engagement is helping this generation think critically about the choices they make in their consumption of media. Many young people have lost a sense of history, on almost all levels. With that comes a detachment from origination of materials and items. In other words, a lot of young people are not really clear on why they

DANIEL WHITE HODGE

Daniel White Hodge, PhD, is the director of the Center for Youth Ministry Studies and associate professor of youth ministry at North Park University in Chicago. Currently, his research and community engagement explore the intersections of faith, critical race theory, justice, hip-hop culture and emerging multiethnic Millennial culture. His three current books are *Heaven Has A Ghetto: The Missiological Gospel & Theology of Tupac Amaru Shakur; The Soul Of Hip-Hop: Rimbs, Timbs & A Cultural Theology;* and *Hip-Hop's Hostile Gospel: A Post Soul Theological Exploration.* He is working on a coauthored book with Irene Cho (Fuller Youth Institute) titled *Between God & Kanye: Youth Ministry in a Post-Civil Rights Era.*

www.WhiteHodge.com

> A LOT OF YOUNG PEOPLE ARE NOT REALLY CLEAR ON WHY THEY DO THE THINGS THEY DO. IT IS IMPERATIVE FOR A MINISTRY TO PROCESS THAT INFORMATION WITH THEM

do the things they do; thus, it is imperative for a ministry to process that information with them. It means getting in the mix and deconstructing music that you might not agree with or even like, but any time spent helping your youth process meaning and their love for that song is important. That does mean, however, that youth workers (both paid and volunteers) need critical skills to interpret what messages are and how they are developed within media. It means doing the difficult work of finding God within the sacred, the profane and the secular, and in turn developing a missional model of engagement, having the gospel at the center, for young people immersed in media.

Q: What unique opportunities does a youth group have to pursue and live out multicultural ministry, perhaps in ways that might prove more difficult among other age groups?

A: I think that the time and era we are in is ripe for engagement with intercultural ministry. I use the term *intercultural* because it is more about the interweaving of cultures into a particular ethos rather than simply having multiple cultures. In other words, it is too simple to have "many cultures" present, without ever interweaving them into the church or ministry. Moreover, interculturalism is about removing hegemonic authority and disrupting dominance from one group. Thus, the term is much more appropriate and applicable.

That said, young people are open and at a place where caring adults are still important in their lives—something that seems to hold true across all studies of youth and adolescents. Therefore, there are myriad spaces to engage interculturalism:

- Partnering with local ministries on excursion trips to places such as Flint, Michigan, or Ferguson, Missouri
- Using current events as a platform for young people to dialogue and engage

- Taking trips to key Civil Rights locations throughout the country
- Making the decision to cultivate interculturalism in the congregation
- Creating games in youth group that replicate what is happening in current events (e.g. rigging Monopoly to illustrate income inequality)
- Inviting organizers and local activists to come talk, or going to them to see what is happening in their context

I think the goal is to get young people involved and talking, being present with them and helping them process issues of interculturalism. You may need some help—especially in homogenous and monoethnic settings, or if you are a youth pastor that has a very conservative senior team. Yet I would argue that these issues are important enough to "die on the hill" for. Young people are ready; more than likely they are already engaged and talking about the issues with their friends. Why not invite that into a space that you can build upon?

Q: There are a handful of notable differences in the ways that urban senior and youth pastors responded to the survey. For example, pastors of urban churches are much more likely to list serving the community and serving the church body as top goals of youth ministry, and less likely to list discipleship and spiritual instruction as their top goal. Urban churches also seem to favor small group or adult-teen mentorship approaches, rather than large group teaching or having teens attend adult services. Do you have any thoughts on how the urban context shapes the perceptions and practices of youth ministry in these ways?

A: I would add that it is not that discipleship is overlooked or not valued, but that, from a traditional youth ministry perspective, it simply looks different. In the urban context, mentoring programs are part of discipleship. There is a sense of lived theology among young people and while there are programmed discipleship spaces, "living life" with young people is seen as a much higher value, as those are typically the learning spaces for youth in those settings.

Because urban spaces are more likely to be smaller than, say, a suburban megachurch youth group, small groups and fewer programmed events are typically what works better. Moreover, the urban context is dealing with pragmatics that the suburban youth pastor might not be aware of or even engaged with. For example, an urban youth worker might have to deal with a young person being harassed by the local police, gang fights in front of their building, a parent on their way to or from prison or a sibling that is missing school to hang out with the local street hustler—all in a day's work. Also, there is sometimes less of a parental presence, and therefore the urban youth worker takes on more of the role of a parent or guardian. When I was doing youth ministry with Urban Young Life in the Bay Area, I ended up acting as a guardian to several young men. I went to PTA meetings, checked grades and at many points provided shelter in times of crisis. These are just some examples of what some suburban youth pastors face only occasionally, if at all.

I would be remiss if I did not mention the *urban* context is changing. Urban is more of a cultural and spatial term rather than an actual geographic term. We have to remember, in cities like Chicago, those in suburban poverty now outnumber those in urban poverty. And with the rise in "redeveloping" central business districts of cities across the U.S., the working class and those at the poverty line are often displaced for more affluent classes. The 'hood is coming to the suburban pastor, and never before has there been such an impetus for the suburban pastor to be trained in intercultural studies and by urban youth

THE 'HOOD IS COMING TO THE SUBURBAN PASTOR. WE ARE BECOMING MORE URBAN, NOT MORE SUBURBAN

workers. We are becoming more urban, not more suburban. It is imperative that the field of youth ministry begins to embrace the richness and value of urban youth work. When seen as a vital part of the new generation of youth ministry development, it can be embraced, rather than just seen as an adjunct to youth ministry programs or training.

WHAT'S NEXT FOR YOUTH MINISTRY

BY DAVID KINNAMAN, PRESIDENT OF BARNA GROUP

What is the state of youth ministry? For the most part, youth ministry in the U.S. is stable and functioning effectively. As our team analyzed the results of more than 2,000 interviews, it became clear that ministry to teenagers in today's local churches is mostly humming along; no dramatic spikes or significant dips are showing up in the data. If youth ministry were a category of stocks in a securities exchange (for the sake of analogy), our recommendation would be to "hold." It's stable, stable, stable.

Even so, the relative health of youth ministry is a point we should not quickly gloss over. Despite all the changes, pressures and expectations heaped onto this area of ministry, the vast majority of paid and volunteer youth workers are doing just fine, thank you. Not that they're on autopilot; our findings indicate most pour their heart and soul into serving young people even as they face frustrations. And despite rumors to the contrary, senior pastors and youth pastors have a reasonably shared view of the purpose and effectiveness of their church's youth ministry. Moreover, both groups of leaders remain hopeful and confident.

In addition, most churchgoing parents of teens find youth ministry to be a helpful and rewarding part of their kids' spiritual lives. We interpret parents' optimistic opinions as additional indicators of youth ministry's vitality.

This report should be a reminder to take stock of all the things that are going right. Even if there are packed schedules to keep, burdensome budgets to balance and difficult conversations to have, consider pausing right now (no, really) and thanking Jesus for the ways he is blessing your ministry. Make a list of things that are working and acknowledge the people who make them work. Then, based on that list, mobilize, motivate and resource to build on what's going right.

In other words, if it ain't broke, don't fix it.

Writing books is endless, and much study wears you out. That's the whole story. Here now is my final conclusion: Fear God and obey his commands, for this is everyone's duty.

ECCLESIASTES 12:12–13

But—you knew there was a *but,* right?—we also have to acknowledge that stability is not necessarily the most effective approach to rapid cultural change. Youth ministry is being forced to operate in a totally new context. The youth landscape is more complex, accelerated and diverse. The social and spiritual lives of adolescents are being reinvented before our eyes.

We need to shift our thinking from merely keeping youth ministry healthy to creating the future of youth ministry. How will we meet the following challenges?

1. **Rising Bible skepticism.** Barna's work on behalf of American Bible Society, published in *The Bible in America,* shows the degree to which Millennials and teens are increasingly skeptical of the Bible. There is growing consensus, especially among young non-Christians, that the Bible is not just irrelevant but that it's actually a dangerous book of dogma used to oppress people. *How can youth ministry equip teens to place greater confidence in the authority of the Bible?*

2. **Increasing loneliness.** Despite the space-age awesomeness of digital tools and the wonderful benefits of social media, Americans are twice as likely today as a decade ago to say they are lonely. And teens are increasingly native to this trend: hyper-connected, yet isolated. Furthermore, our research on discipleship shows that churchgoers tend to believe spiritual growth happens best on their own, rather than in community. *How can youth ministry reverse the isolating trends inside and outside the church, including in teens' digital lives, in order to engage them in deep, life-shaping relationships?*

3. **Pervasive pornography.** Barna's massive study on this subject, *The Porn Phenomenon,* commissioned by Josh McDowell Ministry, illustrates the incredible degree to which porn has

become mainstream and widely accessible. Two findings are especially astonishing: 1) Teens regard not recycling as morally worse than viewing porn, and 2) many talk about porn with their peers as a natural and normal part of human sexuality. Furthermore, many youth leaders admit to personally struggling with porn use. And yet most churches have no program or ministry to help. Our house is engulfed in the flames of ubiquitous sexual content, and we're using water pistols to fight the fire. (Or worse, those tasked with putting out the flames are playing with fire themselves.) *How can youth ministry bring a more robust set of tools to the crisis of pornography, focusing on building sturdier souls and grace-filled communities?*

4. **Confusion regarding human sexuality.** Another major challenge facing today's youth ministry is widespread confusion on matters of human sexuality. A majority of younger practicing Christians continue to hold traditionally orthodox and biblical views on porn, sex outside of marriage and same-sex relationships, yet their views stand in stark contrast to their peers'. The Millennial generation has changed its collective mind on traditional Christian sexual ethics, and the pressure on young Christians to articulate countercultural biblical commitments on these matters is enormous. *How can youth ministry foster a grace-and-truth approach to human sexuality?*

5. **Me-first morality.** Another concerning challenge we must meet is the cultural emergence of a moral code that puts the Self at the center. Gabe Lyons and I document this "new moral code" in the book *Good Faith*, but it is actually not so new (see the last verse of Judges: "people did whatever seemed right in their own eyes"). As a researcher, I was shocked to see the degree to which practicing Christian

Millennials believe "the best way to find yourself is to look within yourself" and "the highest goal of life is to enjoy yourself." *How can youth ministry confront the "me-first" spirit of the age by turning the hearts of teens (and their parents) outward to find themselves in Jesus?*

6. **Pressurized Christian identity.** Young Christians are more likely than older generations of believers to say they feel sidelined, afraid to speak up and concerned about looking stupid. Of course, this is partly the perennial challenge of peer pressure that tends to lessen somewhat with age. Yet the apostle Paul's testimony that "I am not ashamed of this Good News about Christ" is a challenge to every generation. If we peek behind the trends and understand how intense it is to be countercultural as a young person today—to live like Daniel in Babylon—we gain a greater measure of sympathy for teens. *How can youth ministry make a renewed commitment to their development as disciples in "digital Babylon"?*

7. **An era defined by achievement.** One of the key themes of *The State of Youth Ministry* is the degree to which youth pastors struggle with the busyness of today's teens. And the surprise counterpoint: Parents are generally just fine with their kids' busyness. This points to the challenge of making disciples in an era defined by achievement. Most teens expect to land their dream job by age 25. One in four believes they will be famous within the next 10 years. College is no longer a place for character formation but for skills-building and increasing one's earning potential. In response, everything in a teen's life is becoming a résumé builder. And parents are often not only complicit with this drive to succeed but actually behind it. *How can youth ministry promote a biblical view of fame, influence and achievement among teens and parents: that God*

uses ambition, but only to the extent it serves his purposes?
(Ecclesiastes is a good place to start.)

8. **Conversation-challenged disciples.** Barna has found that many Christians struggle to have meaningful conversations with people who are different from them. Evangelicals, in particular, admit they experience conversational obstacles with atheists, Muslims and Mormons, as well as LGBT people. In an increasingly diverse and religiously pluralistic culture, we cannot settle for teenagers to become the same kinds of conversation-challenged disciples. The gospel compels us to be conversation-enabled, especially with people who are different from us (see Colossians 4:5–6). *How can youth ministry train young people to be some of the best conversationalists on the planet, for the purposes of Christ and his glory?*

These are just a handful of the challenges—and remarkable opportunities—coming to a youth ministry near you. If right now you're feeling a sense of hopeful excitement and a desire to dive in and address these realities, your call for youth ministry is as strong as ever!

TOWARD A DEEPER VISION OF DISCIPLESHIP

While nationwide trends can provide helpful insights, each leader is an individual serving a unique community of faith in a specific neighborhood. It matters little that a majority of churches in America increased their youth budget if your church is not in the majority. But accurate information *can* be a useful tool for wise decision-making and planning for the future of disciple-making.

Barna's data-gathering over the past decade has led us to believe there are five key components to instilling in teens a faith that keeps them connected to God and his church into young adulthood. These are: 1) a meaningful mentoring relationship with at least one Christian adult who isn't their parent; 2) learning cultural discernment, the ability to apply faith to their everyday reality; 3) reverse mentoring, an opportunity to share their knowledge and skills with others, especially older adults; 4) vocational discipleship, an understanding of their career choices as an expression of God's calling on their lives; and 5) a personal experience of Jesus.

Data can be a conversational jumping-off point that leads to deeper thinking about how churches disciple teens and equip parents in the project of faith formation. Keeping the five components of lasting faith in mind, here are some conversations you and your team of fellow leaders and engaged parents might have, based on the research in *The State of Youth Ministry*:

- How do we define discipleship in our church? How do we measure effective discipleship based on our definition?
- Is youth ministry a right-sized priority for our church? Should it play a bigger role in our overall mission? If so, how?
- How can we connect adults and teens in mentoring friendships that bless and grow both?
- How does teen busyness impact effective discipleship? Can we cast a more compelling vision for parents to make church a higher priority in their teen's life?
- Do we need to reconsider the priority of reaching out to unchurched teens? How can we equip church youth to be effective evangelists?
- Why do we engage in service and missions projects? How do we measure success when it comes to teen service?
- Are we hopeful about the future of our youth ministry? If so, what decisions can we make to ensure those hopes become reality? If not, what needs to change?

It is our prayer that this report informs and equips you to joyfully obey as you walk alongside teens in the footsteps of Jesus.

APPENDIX

A. DATA TABLES

SENIOR PASTORS

What priority do you place on youth programs, relative to other ministries? Is this...	% All Senior Pastors	Church Location			Church Size			Church Ethnicity	
		% URBAN	% SUBURBAN	% SMALL TOWN / RURAL	% 1 TO 199	% 200 TO 499	% 500+	% WHITE	% ALL NON-WHITE
The number one priority						1			1
Among the top three priorities	73	82	74	68	73	75	69	69	90
Important, but not one of the top three priorities	27	18	25	32	27	24	31	31	9
Not something you are focused on at this time			1						

How much do you think the quality of your youth ministry impacts your overall church attendance? In other words, do you believe youth ministry retains or attracts families?	% All Senior Pastors	Church Location			Church Size			Church Ethnicity	
		% URBAN	% SUBURBAN	% SMALL TOWN / RURAL	% 1 TO 199	% 200 TO 499	% 500+	% WHITE	% ALL NON-WHITE
Significant impact	36	34	38	36	33	40	52	36	37
Somewhat of an impact	56	62	55	54	58	51	47	54	61
Not much of an impact	8	4	8	10	9	8	1	10	2

SENIOR PASTORS

When you think about your church's ministry to youth, what are the top two goals? Select only two.	% All Senior Pastors	Church Location			Church Size			Church Ethnicity	
		% URBAN	% SUBURBAN	% SMALL TOWN / RURAL	% 1 TO 199	% 200 TO 499	% 500+	% WHITE	% ALL NON-WHITE
Discipleship / spiritual instruction	71	48	77	76	70	70	74	74	54
Building relationships with youth	40	33	36	45	40	40	33	42	26
Evangelism and outreach to youth	29	30	29	29	26	43	26	31	23
Getting parents more involved in their youth's spiritual formation	18	22	19	16	17	20	26	16	26
Serving the community	17	31	17	12	20	7	20	14	35
Providing a safe and nurturing environment	12	10	15	10	14	9	3	12	11
Evangelism and outreach to parents of teens	7	7	4	9	6	7	17	7	5
Serving the church body	6	18	1	3	7	4		3	20
Other			1				1	1	

YOUTH PASTORS

When you think about your church's ministry to youth, what are the top two goals? Select only two.	% All Youth Pastors	Church Location			Church Size			Church Ethnicity	
		% URBAN	% SUBURBAN	% SMALL TOWN / RURAL	% 1 TO 199	% 200 TO 499	% 500+	% WHITE	% ALL NON-WHITE
Discipleship / spiritual instruction	75	59	76	84	77	74	75	78	58
Building relationships with youth	48	55	44	46	44	49	50	46	54
Evangelism and outreach to youth	24	18	31	20	23	23	28	24	26
Getting parents more involved in their youth's spiritual formation	23	25	21	25	19	27	22	25	17
Serving the community	10	16	10	5	17	6	7	8	18
Providing a safe and nurturing environment	10	8	10	10	11	7	12	10	8
Evangelism and outreach to parents of teens	4	7	2	4	3	5	3	4	5
Serving the church body	4	10	2	2	2	8		3	7
Other	1		3	1	3		3	1	3

SENIOR PASTORS

Do you feel your church is more effective at...? Slide the marker to indicate where your strength is between these two objectives.	% All Senior Pastors	Church Location			Church Size			Church Ethnicity	
		% URBAN	% SUBURBAN	% SMALL TOWN / RURAL	% 1 TO 199	% 200 TO 499	% 500+	% WHITE	% ALL NON-WHITE
Reaching teenagers outside of the church	1	1	1	1	1			1	
[Somewhat] Reaching teenagers outside of the church	17	21	19	14	16	18	26	16	24
[Somewhat] Discipling teens who are already part of the church family	64	65	61	65	62	69	64	65	59
Discipling teens who are already part of the church family	18	13	19	20	20	12	10	18	18

YOUTH PASTORS

Do you feel your church is more effective at...? Slide the marker to indicate where your strength is between these two objectives.	% All Youth Pastors	Church Location			Church Size			Church Ethnicity	
		% URBAN	% SUBURBAN	% SMALL TOWN / RURAL	% 1 TO 199	% 200 TO 499	% 500+	% WHITE	% ALL NON-WHITE
Reaching teenagers outside of the church	2	3	3		2	2	2	2	4
[Somewhat] Reaching teenagers outside of the church	12	9	12	14	7	14	14	12	10
[Somewhat] Discipling teens who are already part of the church family	56	57	57	53	59	56	50	56	56
Discipling teens who are already part of the church family	30	31	29	32	32	27	34	31	30

SENIOR PASTORS

Which of the following programs or formats does your church youth ministry use or offer regularly? Select all that apply. (See p. 105 for parents' answers.)	% All Senior Pastors	Church Location			Church Size			Church Ethnicity	
		% URBAN	% SUBURBAN	% SMALL TOWN / RURAL	% 1 TO 199	% 200 TO 499	% 500+	% WHITE	% ALL NON-WHITE
Youth attendance in main church worship service	87	77	90	89	86	90	81	90	71
Social activities	84	82	81	87	84	89	77	86	73
Small discipleship or Bible study groups	79	80	77	80	78	86	66	78	84
Youth conferences	54	56	51	56	51	59	71	56	46
Large group teaching	49	35	52	52	41	61	90	55	19
Large group worship	30	36	26	31	23	44	70	30	31
Small prayer groups	29	48	22	26	24	38	58	24	52
Adult-teen mentoring programs	25	36	24	22	21	34	45	24	33
Mission trips / service projects	4	1	4	5	4	6	2	5	
Other	3	4	2	4	3	4	4	3	2

YOUTH PASTORS

Which of the following programs or formats does your church youth ministry use or offer regularly? Select all that apply. (See p. 105 for parents' answers.)	% All Youth Pastors	Church Location			Church Size			Church Ethnicity	
		% URBAN	% SUBURBAN	% SMALL TOWN / RURAL	% 1 TO 199	% 200 TO 499	% 500+	% WHITE	% ALL NON-WHITE
Youth attendance in main church worship service	84	71	85	90	84	82	86	87	68
Social activities	85	76	93	81	82	87	85	86	78
Small discipleship or Bible study groups	80	77	84	78	78	82	79	82	74
Youth conferences	56	59	53	58	60	55	54	55	60
Large group teaching	71	62	76	71	64	67	86	74	55
Large group worship	48	37	53	49	34	43	73	49	43
Small prayer groups	23	32	20	19	23	23	22	21	31
Adult-teen mentoring programs	23	25	24	22	14	30	24	24	20
Other	4	2	3	7	7	3	3	5	
Mission trips / service projects	6	5	9	4	5	6	8	8	
Leadership training	1	1	2		1	1		1	
Retreats / camps	2	1	2	2	1	3	1	2	2

If you had to choose, which of these would be the preferred format for youth activities in your church? Slide the marker to indicate where your preference is between these two objectives.	% All Youth Pastors	Church Location			Church Size			Church Ethnicity	
		% URBAN	% SUBURBAN	% SMALL TOWN / RURAL	% 1 TO 199	% 200 TO 499	% 500+	% WHITE	% ALL NON-WHITE
Large group worship, teaching and / or fellowship activities	5	3	7	4	7	2	8	5	5
[Somewhat] Large group worship, teaching and / or fellowship activities	24	24	26	22	18	25	31	24	24
[Somewhat] Small group discipleship, teaching and / or mentoring programs	53	51	52	55	57	55	44	54	49
Small group discipleship, teaching and / or mentoring programs	18	22	15	19	17	19	17	17	22

At your church, how much significance is placed on reaching teenagers outside of the church?	% All Youth Pastors	Church Location			Church Size			Church Ethnicity	
		% URBAN	% SUBURBAN	% SMALL TOWN / RURAL	% 1 TO 199	% 200 TO 499	% 500+	% WHITE	% ALL NON-WHITE
A lot	13	8	14	15	9	14	16	11	22
Some	41	42	42	39	38	43	41	40	44
A little	37	38	36	38	42	36	34	40	25
None at all	9	13	7	8	12	7	9	9	10

How much emphasis is put on discipleship of students inside the church?	% All Youth Pastors	Church Location			Church Size			Church Ethnicity	
		% URBAN	% SUBURBAN	% SMALL TOWN / RURAL	% 1 TO 199	% 200 TO 499	% 500+	% WHITE	% ALL NON-WHITE
A strong emphasis	45	25	54	47	42	49	42	49	28
A moderate emphasis	40	56	32	38	40	37	43	36	56
Not enough of an emphasis	15	19	14	15	18	15	14	15	16

In the past two years, has your church participated in a youth service project, meaning a service or mission project specifically designed for middle and / or high school students?	% All Youth Pastors	Church Location			Church Size			Church Ethnicity	
		% URBAN	% SUBURBAN	% SMALL TOWN / RURAL	% 1 TO 199	% 200 TO 499	% 500+	% WHITE	% ALL NON-WHITE
Yes	88	79	94	87	87	89	86	90	79
No	10	19	5	11	10	10	12	9	18
Not sure	2	2	1	3	3	1	3	2	3

Do any of these describe the goal(s) of a youth service or mission trip? Please select the top three. (See p. 115 to compare with parent goals.)	% All Youth Pastors	Church Location			Church Size			Church Ethnicity	
		% URBAN	% SUBURBAN	% SMALL TOWN / RURAL	% 1 TO 199	% 200 TO 499	% 500+	% WHITE	% ALL NON-WHITE
Loving and serving others	73	70	71	78	75	71	77	77	56
Being the "hands and feet of Jesus"	56	40	60	63	43	58	69	60	41
Discipleship opportunities with the youth participating	41	45	41	39	42	42	38	40	45
Outreach or evangelism to the people or organization you are serving	36	30	37	40	39	38	30	38	28
Teaching and modeling compassion to the youth	30	33	33	23	25	33	30	28	36
Participating in responses to systemic injustice and / or advocating for social justice	15	25	15	8	15	13	17	14	18
Providing for the poor	15	19	13	14	22	13	10	12	28
An opportunity for youth to "see the world"	12	12	11	13	17	6	17	11	16
Outreach or evangelism to the youth participating	11	17	11	8	12	14	5	10	17
Other	1		1	1	2			1	

Here are a few descriptions of youth service projects or trips. For each, please indicate how appealing, if at all, each would be to your church. (% "very appealing")	% All Youth Pastors	Church Location			Church Size			Church Ethnicity	
		% URBAN	% SUBURBAN	% SMALL TOWN / RURAL	% 1 TO 199	% 200 TO 499	% 500+	% WHITE	% ALL NON-WHITE
An experience where students experience growth in their faith-development.	82	74	86	83	86	81	81	84	72
An experience where students meet real needs and make a difference in a community.	77	62	84	78	72	79	80	79	68
An experience where students are able to spread the good news of Jesus through evangelism.	54	55	52	54	60	51	51	50	69

PARENTS

How often does your teen attend your church's youth ministry programs? (among parents whose teen attends church with them)	% Church-Attending Christians	% Non-Christians
Several times a week	21	52
Once a week	42	39
Once or twice a month	16	2
Less often	13	2
Never	9	6

Does your teen ever attend youth ministry programs at a church? (among non-Christian parents)	% Non-Christians
Yes, once a week	5
Yes, once or twice a month	6
Yes, less often	6
No, never	82

Note: All remaining questions asked among parents who are familiar with the youth program and whose teen regularly attends.

How effective do you feel your teen's youth ministry program is at ministering to youth? If your teen attends programs at multiple churches, please rate your church. If your teen does not attend youth ministry programs where you attend church, please rate the church they attend most often.	% Church-Attending Christians	% Non-Christians
Very effective	51	63
Somewhat effective	43	29
Not that effective	6	8
Not at all effective	1	

How satisfied are you with your teen's youth ministry program? Again, if your teen attends programs at multiple churches, please rate your church. If your teen does not attend youth ministry programs where you attend church, please rate the church they attend most often.	% Church-Attending Christians	% Non-Christians
Very satisfied	57	60
Somewhat satisfied	40	39
Not too satisfied	3	1
Not at all satisfied	1	

Which of the following programs or formats does your teen's youth ministry offer regularly? Select all that apply. (See pp. 96–97 for senior pastors' and youth pastors' answers.)	% Church-Attending Christians	% Non-Christians
Social activities	61	64
Small discipleship or Bible study groups	49	38
Small prayer groups	44	50
Youth attendance in main church worship service	43	53
Youth conferences	42	23
Large group youth-specific worship	35	23
Large group teaching	33	17
Large group worship	31	35
Adult-teen mentoring programs	29	20
Not sure	1	5
Other	1	

Below are some factors that parents may or may not expect of youth ministry programs. How important are each of these factors to you?		% Church-Attending Christians	% Non-Christians
An environment where your teen feels safe to explore faith	Very important	70	65
	Somewhat important	27	27
	Not too important	1	8
	Not sure	2	
Positive peer relationships	Very important	68	62
	Somewhat important	29	29
	Not too important	3	4
	Not at all important		5
	Not sure	1	
A place where they can bring their friends	Very important	57	62
	Somewhat important	29	36
	Not too important	13	2
	Not at all important		
	Not sure	1	
Opportunities for your teen to participate in service or mission projects	Very important	48	52
	Somewhat important	36	33
	Not too important	15	16
	Not at all important		
	Not sure	1	

Below are some factors that parents may or may not expect of youth ministry programs. How important are each of these factors to you?		% Church-Attending Christians	% Non-Christians
A variety of activities	Very important	51	68
	Somewhat important	46	29
	Not too important	2	2
	Not at all important		
	Not sure	1	
Mentoring or discipleship is a key part of the program	Very important	52	54
	Somewhat important	40	29
	Not too important	7	12
	Not at all important		5
	Not sure	1	
Guidance for future career / direction in life	Very important	56	53
	Somewhat important	35	42
	Not too important	6	6
	Not at all important	1	
	Not sure	1	
Outreach to teens in the community that do not presently attend church	Very important	47	65
	Somewhat important	40	33
	Not too important	10	2
	Not at all important	1	
	Not sure	2	

How would you rate your teen's youth program on each of the following factors?		% Church-Attending Christians	% Non-Christians
An environment where your teen feels safe to explore faith	Very strong	52	57
	Somewhat strong	39	37
	Somewhat weak	6	
	Very weak	1	6
	Not sure	2	
	Not applicable	1	
A place where they can bring their friends	Very strong	49	66
	Somewhat strong	36	29
	Somewhat weak	11	
	Not sure	2	5
	Not applicable	1	
Positive peer relationships	Very strong	48	68
	Somewhat strong	46	13
	Somewhat weak	3	17
	Very weak	1	2
	Not sure	1	
	Not applicable	1	
A variety of activities	Very strong	46	56
	Somewhat strong	38	29
	Somewhat weak	13	16
	Very weak	1	
	Not sure	1	
	Not applicable	1	

How would you rate your teen's youth program on each of the following factors?		% Church-Attending Christians	% Non-Christians
Opportunities for your teen to participate in service or mission projects	Very strong	40	42
	Somewhat strong	39	42
	Somewhat weak	17	8
	Very weak	1	7
	Not sure	1	1
	Not applicable	1	
Mentoring or discipleship is a key part of the program	Very strong	36	56
	Somewhat strong	42	19
	Somewhat weak	13	17
	Very weak	1	5
	Not sure	7	3
	Not applicable	1	
Guidance for future career / direction in life	Very strong	39	44
	Somewhat strong	36	45
	Somewhat weak	14	10
	Very weak	2	
	Not sure	7	1
	Not applicable	3	
Outreach to teens in the community that do not presently attend church	Very strong	38	69
	Somewhat strong	32	16
	Somewhat weak	17	13
	Very weak	7	
	Not sure	4	2
	Not applicable	3	

Below are various expectations parents can have for their teen's youth leader. Please rate your expectation of your teen's youth leader.		% Church-Attending Christians	% Non-Christians
Discipling; helping teens grow more spiritually mature	Major expectation	43	55
	Minor expectation	32	35
	Not an expectation	17	7
	Not sure	8	3
Talking to teens about sexuality and dating	Major expectation	39	51
	Minor expectation	36	41
	Not an expectation	20	8
	Not sure	6	
Warning them about drugs and alcohol	Major expectation	59	50
	Minor expectation	29	30
	Not an expectation	9	21
	Not sure	3	
Helping them use media in a safe way	Major expectation	39	52
	Minor expectation	43	24
	Not an expectation	15	25
	Not sure	4	

Below are various expectations parents can have for their teen's youth leader. Please rate your expectation of your teen's youth leader.		% Church-Attending Christians	% Non-Christians
Helping them navigate family relationships	Major expectation	62	54
	Minor expectation	30	35
	Not an expectation	5	11
	Not sure	3	
Helping them navigate friend relationships	Major expectation	61	63
	Minor expectation	34	30
	Not an expectation	2	2
	Not sure	3	5
Helping them determine a career	Major expectation	33	56
	Minor expectation	30	30
	Not an expectation	30	7
	Not sure	7	7

Have you had any personal interaction with your teen's youth leader?	% Church-Attending Christians	% Non-Christians
A lot	43	55
Some	32	35
A little / not much	17	7
None	8	3

How important is it to you for your teen to participate in volunteer or community service experiences?	% Church-Attending Christians	% Non-Christians	% Non-Attending Christians
Very important	51	39	17
Somewhat important	39	23	62
Not so important	9	17	18
Not at all important	2	22	3

How important would you say extra-curricular activities are in comparison to participating in a church youth group? Please move the slider below to indicate your opinion.	% Church-Attending Christians	% Non-Christians	% Non-Attending Christians
Extra-curricular activities are much more important	3	6	11
Extra-curricular activities are somewhat more important	7	13	19
They are equally important	53	68	61
Church youth group is somewhat more important	27	13	8
Church youth group is much more important	11		2

Has your teen ever participated in a service or mission project with their youth ministry program?	% Church-Attending Christians	% Non-Christians
Yes	53	80
No	45	14
Not sure	2	5

Is there any particular reason why your teen has not participated in a service or mission project through their youth group? Select all that apply.	% Church-Attending Christians
Their youth ministry program has not offered any such opportunity.	35
We just haven't thought about it.	32
He / she is not interested.	28
He / she has too many other commitments.	18
I did not feel comfortable with my teen participating in any of the service or mission projects their youth ministry program offered.	16
My teen already volunteers or serves elsewhere.	7
Other	3

Do any of these describe your goal(s) for a youth service or mission trip? Please select the top three. (See p. 100 to compare with youth pastor goals.)	% Church-Attending Christians	% Non-Christians
Loving and serving others	57	53
Being the "hands and feet of Jesus"	40	15
Teaching and modeling compassion to the youth	33	23
Providing for the poor	30	39
Outreach or evangelism to the people or organization you are serving	18	18
Outreach or evangelism to the youth participating	18	26
An opportunity for youth to "see the world"	25	27
Discipleship opportunities with the youth participating	12	10
Participating in responses to systemic injustice and/or advocating for social justice	13	24

B: DEFINITIONS

U.S. PARENTS OF TEENS 13–17

Self-identified Christian: Identify as a Christian.

Self-identified Catholic: Identify as Christian and as Catholic.

Self-identified Protestant: Identify as Christian and as Protestant.

Non-Christian: Identify as not having any religious faith or a faith other than Christianity.

Church-Attending Christian: Self-identified Christian who has attended a worship service within the past year.

Non-Attending Christian: Self-identified Christian who has not attended a worship service within the past year.

Teen regularly attends youth group: Report their child attends once a week or more often.

Low income: Annual income before taxes is less than $50,000.

Middle income: Annual income before taxes is $50,000 to $99,999.

High income: Annual income before taxes is $100,000 or more.

U.S. PROTESTANT PASTORS

Mainline: Selected one of the following as their denomination: American Baptist, United Church of Christ, Episcopal, Lutheran (Evangelical, ELCA), United Methodist or Presbyterian Church USA (PCUSA).

Non-mainline: All other denominations.

Small church: Adult church attendance on a typical weekend is 199 or less.

Medium church: Adult church attendance on a typical weekend is 200 to 499.

Large church: Adult church attendance on a typical weekend is 500 or more.

Paid youth leader: Church employs at least one part- or full-time ministry staff person dedicated to youth ministry.

Region: Church is located in one of four major U.S. regions: Northeast, South, Midwest or West.

Location: Church's neighborhood is urban, suburban, small town or rural.

Church ethnicity: Church's membership is primarily white, black or Hispanic.

YOUTH PASTORS

Small youth group: Teen attendance at weekly youth activities is 50 or less.

Large youth group: Teen attendance at weekly youth activities is 51 or more.

C. METHODOLOGIES

The data contained in this report originated through research conducted by Barna Group of Ventura, California. Youth Specialties and YouthWorks commissioned the studies.

This report is based on data gathered from a total of five surveys with U.S. parents of teenagers, senior pastors of U.S. Protestant churches and youth pastors of U.S. Protestant churches. Of these surveys, two were conducted in Fall 2013 and the remaining three were conducted in Spring 2016.

2016 METHODOLOGY

PARENTS

The study among U.S. parents was conducted online with a random sample of 606 U.S. adults with children ages 13 to 19. The survey was fielded March 29 through April 7, 2016, and is representative of the U.S. parent population. Sampling error for this data is plus or minus 4 percentage points at the 95-percent confidence level.

SENIOR PASTORS

A total of 381 senior pastors of U.S. Protestant churches across 50 states were surveyed online March 15 to June 7, 2016. Respondents were recruited via two sample sources: Barna Group's senior pastor panel (n=299) and a random sample of Protestant pastors obtained from a public listing of churches (n=82). These data were minimally weighted to be representative of U.S. Protestant churches by region, size and denomination. The sampling error for the senior pastor survey is plus or minus 5 percentage points at the 95-percent confidence level.

A total of 352 youth pastors of U.S. Protestant churches across 50 states were surveyed online March 15 to June 15, 2016. These participants were recruited from two sources: through members of Barna Group's panel of senior pastors (n=51) and a random sample of youth pastors obtained from a public listing of churches and youth pastors (n=301). These data were minimally weighted by region and denomination to be representative of U.S. Protestant churches with youth ministries. The sampling error for the youth pastor data is plus or minus 5 percentage points at the 95-percent confidence level.

2013 METHODOLOGY

SENIOR PASTORS

Senior pastor data from 2013 was collected via Barna's Pastor-Poll[SM] which consisted of 601 telephone interviews conducted among a representative sample of senior pastors of Protestant churches within the continental U.S. The telephone interviews were conducted from September 20 to October 9, 2013. The sampling error for the PastorPoll[SM] is plus or minus 4 percentage points at the 95-percent confidence level.

Survey calls were made at various times during the day, Monday through Friday, so that every individual selected for inclusion was contacted up to five separate days, at different times of the day, to maximize the possibility of contact. Regional, denominational and adult worship attendance quotas based on national data sources were designed to ensure the final group of pastors interviewed reflected the distribution of churches nationwide.

YOUTH PASTORS

This study included online surveys with a randomly selected sample of 463 youth pastors nationwide. The survey was conducted October 7 to October 25, 2013. These data were minimally weighted by region and denomination to be representative of U.S. Protestant churches with youth ministries. The sampling error for the data is plus or minus 4.6 percentage points at the 95-percent confidence level.

D: ACKNOWLEDGEMENTS

Barna Group offers our sincere thanks to our partners at Youth Specialties and YouthWorks.

Barna also wishes to thank the contributors to *The State of Youth Ministry*, Sharon Galgay Ketcham, Terry Linhart, Kara Powell and Daniel White Hodge. Your lives and work are testimonies to God's life-giving Spirit who transforms teens and young adults into the image of Christ, and we are thankful for the insights you've offered here for how the Church can help.

The research team for this study is Brooke Hempell and Josh Pearce. David Kinnaman and Mark Matlock contributed analysis and project leadership. Under the editorial direction of Roxanne Stone, Alyce Youngblood and Aly Hawkins wrote *The State of Youth Ministry*. Chaz Russo created the cover and data visualizations, and Rob Williams designed the report, including all charts, graphs and data tables. Brenda Usery managed production.

The State of Youth Ministry team thanks our Barna colleagues Amy Brands, Chrisandra Bolton, Matt Carobini, Joyce Chiu, Inga Dahlstedt, Bill Denzel, Traci Hochmuth, Pam Jacob, Jill Kinnaman, Elaine Klautzsch, Cory Maxwell-Coghlan, Steve McBeth, Elise Miller, Megan Pritchett, Caitlin Schuman, Todd Sorenson, Sara Tandon and Todd White.

E: ABOUT THE RESEARCH PARTNERS

Barna Group is a research firm dedicated to providing action-able insights on faith and culture, with a particular focus on the Christian church. In its 32-year history, Barna Group has conducted more than one million interviews in the course of hundreds of studies, and has become a go-to source for organizations that want to better understand a complex and changing world from a faith perspective. Barna's clients include a broad range of academic institutions, churches, non-profits and businesses, such as Alpha, the Templeton Foundation, Pepperdine University, Fuller Seminary, the Bill and Melinda Gates Foundation, the Maclellan Foundation, DreamWorks Animation, Focus Features, Habitat for Humanity, the Navigators, NBC-Universal, the ONE Campaign, Paramount Pictures, the Salvation Army, Walden Media, Sony and World Vision. The firm's studies are frequently quoted by major media outlets such as *The Economist*, BBC, CNN, *USA Today*, the *Wall Street Journal*, Fox News, *Huffington Post*, the *New York Times* and the *Los Angeles Times*. *www.Barna.com*

Youth Specialties equips and encourages churches to help teenagers find and follow Jesus by creating resources, convening youth workers at events and providing training. For more than 40 years, Youth Specialties has served as an international thought leader in Christian youth ministry. Today, Youth Specialties serves more than 100,000 youth workers worldwide each year through training seminars, conventions, books, curriculum and online resources. *www.YouthSpecialties.com*

YouthWorks exists to connect teenagers to God, each other and communities through life-changing, Christ-centered mission trips. For more than 20 years, YouthWorks has seen short-term trips lead to long-term impact for teenagers and communities. And for YouthWorks, both are mission-critical. Each summer, more than 25,000 students, adults and families from 1,500 churches partner with more than 70 communities across North America. YouthWorks is committed to providing high-quality experiences that broaden perspectives, ignite passions, expose possibilities and inspire pursuits.

www.YouthWorks.com